THE ISLE OF MAN
A WALKER'S GUIDE

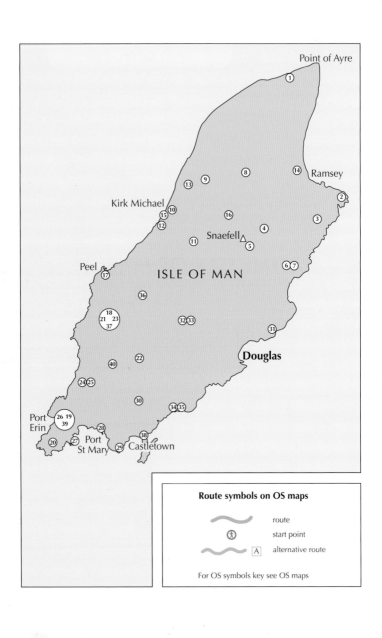

Point of Ayre

Ramsey

Kirk Michael

Snaefell △

Peel

ISLE OF MAN

Douglas

Port
Erin

Port
St Mary

Castletown

THE ISLE OF MAN
A WALKER'S GUIDE

by
Terry Marsh

CICERONE

2 POLICE SQUARE, MILNTHORPE, CUMBRIA LA7 7PY
www.cicerone.co.uk

© Terry Marsh 2004
ISBN-10: 1 85284 399 3
ISBN-13: 978 1 85284 399 1
Reprinted 2006, 2008
A catalogue record for this book is available from the British Library.

Photos by the author

ols Ordnance Survey® This product includes mapping data licensed from Ordnance Survey® with the permission of the Controller of Her Majesty's Stationery Office. © Crown copyright 2003. All rights reserved. Licence number PU100012932

To Vivienne, who walked them all with me, come rain or shine.

Acknowledgements

In particular I acknowledge the generous support given to me by the Isle of Man Department of Tourism. I must also place on record my great indebtedness to Daphne Caine and Howard Grundey, both of whom kindly read the manuscript for me, corrected my mistakes and offered many helpful suggestions. Any errors that remain are mine and not theirs.

Advice to Readers

Readers are advised that while every effort is taken by the author to ensure the accuracy of this guidebook, changes can occur which may affect the contents. It is advisable to check locally on transport, accommodation, shops, etc, but even rights of way can be altered. Paths can be affected by forestry work, landslip or changes of ownership.

The author would welcome information on any updates and changes. Please send to: terrymarsh@wpu.org.uk

Front cover: Bradda Hill seen from the slopes of Lhiattee ny Beinnee

CONTENTS

INTRODUCTION

For most people, the Isle of Man is an enigma. Most often heard, sadly, is the comment 'I've always wanted to go, but never got round to it'.

Few would think of the island as a walker's paradise – yet it is, as this book will demonstrate. Fewer still know anything about the island, save that it has an annual motorcycle race of some severity, that it is something of a tax haven, that Manx cats have no tails, and (I'm pushing it now) the island's bishop has the title 'Bishop of Sodor and Man'. Very few indeed could explain the way the island is governed: is it part of Britain? (No); the United Kingdom? (No); the Commonwealth, then? (Yes). Yet, the Isle of Man is at the very centre (give or take) of the British Isles, roughly equidistant from the other countries. Indeed, they say that on a clear day it is possible to see seven kingdoms: England, Scotland, Wales, Ireland, Man, and the kingdoms of Heaven and the Sea.

The name of the island has some interesting derivations. Julius Caesar mentions an island 'In the middle of the Channel' (by which he meant the Irish Sea), which he called 'Mona', a name also associated with Anglesey, off the Welsh coast. This confusion wasn't eased when Pliny the Elder, writing in AD 74, listed the islands between Britain and Ireland, and

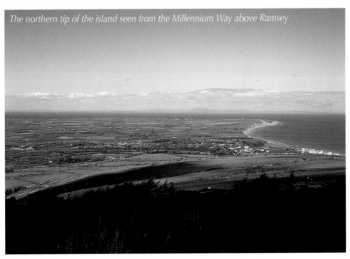

The northern tip of the island seen from the Millennium Way above Ramsey

Above Sulby Reservoir

included Mona, by which he probably meant Anglesey, and Monapia,
which is thought to have been the Isle
of Man. Paulus Orosius (c AD 400)
refers to 'Menavia', a place 'of no
mean size, with fertile soil, inhabited
by a tribe of Scots'. The geographer
who visited Britain at the time of
Hadrian called the island
'Monaoida', while an Irish monk,
Nennius (AD 858) refers to 'Eubonia'.
Later still, the Irish and Welsh forms
become more consistently used,
'Mannan' and 'Mannaw' respec-
tively. The first name-form occurring
on the island is on a runic cross in
Kirk Michael, 'Maun'. Today, it is
known as 'Mannin', 'Vannin' or
'Ellan Vannin', the island of Man.
Those of a more romantic inclination,
however, will opt for the view that

the name refers to a Celtic sea god,
Manannan, the equivalent of the
Roman sea god, Neptune, or the
Greek, Poseidon.

LOCATION AND GENERAL INFORMATION

An island in the Irish Sea, situated
mid-way between England, Scotland,
Ireland and Wales, the Isle of Man
has a land mass of some 572 sq km
(221 sq miles) and measures, at its
extremities, 52km (32⅓ miles) by
22km (13⅔ miles). Geographically it
is part of the British Isles, a depen-
dency of the British crown, but not
part of the United Kingdom. The capital is Douglas, and other towns of
size are Ramsey, Peel and
Castletown. Government of the island

is through the 24 representatives of the House of Keys and a nine-member legislative council, which together make up the Court of Tynwald (the oldest surviving parliamentary body in continuous existence in the world), passing laws subject to the royal assent. Laws passed at Westminster only affect the island if adopted by Tynwald.

The principal industries are light engineering, agriculture, fishing, tourism, banking and insurance. The island, which has a population of 76,315 (2001), produces its own coins and notes in UK currency denominations, and while UK money can be used on the island, Manx notes are not always readily accepted in the UK. The language is English, though there is a true Manx language, closer to Scottish than Irish Gaelic, which almost died out last century but which has increased in popularity recently. Today, Manx Gaelic is spoken by 2.2 per cent of the total population, a figure which rises to 6.5 per cent in the north of the island.

What the island lacks in size it makes up for in its variety of scenery, which reflects almost every type of landscape found elsewhere in the British Isles, from open moorland to thickly wooded glens, sandy beaches to bare mountain tops. The principal rivers are the Santon, the Silver Burn, the Neb-Thenass, the Sulby and the Dhoo and Glass (ie Douglas). Within the 160km (99 miles) of coastline lies a central range of mountains and hills running north-easterly/south-westerly, from which well-defined valleys descend to cliffs and sheltered bays. In the north of the island the landscape is flat and crossed by slow-moving rivers and streams that debouche onto long sandy beaches. Cutting obliquely across the island, generally at right angles to the main axis, is a central valley with Peel at its western end and Douglas at its eastern.

The watershed, or water-parting, which follows the north-east/south-west axis has long been important as the fundamental line of separation of the island into the Northside and the Southside – though this is not the division used in this book, which settles for the much more prosaic division based on maps used during research. Traditionally, Northside has included the 'sheadings' (districts) of Glenfaba, Michael and Ayre, while Southside embraced Garff, Middle and Rushen sheadings. Changes in 1796 modified the original pattern by making Northside include Michael, Ayre and Garff, and Southside, Glenfaba, Rushen and Middle – a more geographically accurate division.

HISTORY AND CULTURE

The earliest evidence for man's settlement on the island comes from the mesolithic period, a time when, quite probably, the island still formed part of the British 'mainland'. By neolithic times (about 4000–4500 years ago),

Man was an island, and its people living around the coastal plains in areas that were covered by predominantly oak woodlands.

During the Bronze Age (c 2000 BC), trade in gold ornaments and bronze artefacts extended across Europe, and the Isle of Man clearly played a part in this trade. Towards the end of this period, the climate changed noticeably and for a while the development of the island slowed down, only regaining momentum with the development of Christianity. This was a time when the Romans populated much of Britain, though they never occupied Man, in spite of the probability that they must have passed close to it en

Rushen Abbey

route with supplies for the garrison manning Hadrian's Wall.

Close contact with Man and the Atlantic coast of Britain continued after the Romans had retreated. During this time, between the 5th and 8th centuries, it is probable that the Isle of Man featured in the itineraries of many Christian missionaries. St Bridget, St Ninian, St Patrick, St Columba and St Cuthbert all figure in church dedications on the island, so it is not too fanciful to suppose that they must have arrived here at some time during their lifetimes.

The scene altered significantly with the conquest of the island by Vikings. This brought about many changes in ethnic make-up, religion and cultural identity. Although pagan at the outset, the Norse quickly succumbed to the influence of Christianity and this, in turn, fostered the propagation of a unique blend of Celtic and Norse influences. The most notable survivor from this period is the Norse annual open-air assembly, the *thing*, at which new laws were announced and disputes settled. In the Norse language, the place for a meeting was a *vollr*, hence Thing-vollr, has become Tynwald, the island's unique focus of government.

During this Scandinavian period the Isle of Man became the capital of an island realm – the Kingdom of the Isles – that embraced all the Hebrides, ruled by a Manx king subordinate to Norwegian sovereignty, with its headquarters on St Patrick's

Isle, today linked to Peel by a causeway. In a religious context, this became known as Ecclesia Sodorensis, a separate diocese, its name based on the Norse for Man and the Hebrides ('the Southern Isles'). In 1266, the Hebrides were ceded to Scotland, heralding the political break-up of the Kingdom of the Isles, but the religious ties continued for much longer and, though long since severed, there is a reminder of this past regime in the title of the Manx bishop of Sodor and Man.

For over 100 years sovereignty of the Isle of Man was disputed between the English and the Scots, with the former ultimately gaining control in 1405 when sovereignty was granted to Sir John Stanley. His descendants – Earls of Derby and Dukes of Atholl – ruled Man for over 300 years, bringing a period of consolidation during which the island became increasingly isolated. This enabled the development of its own form of government, language and personal names. Trade was not encouraged, indeed strictly regulated, and visitors were kept away. The language of the people was Manx – though the well-to-do and government officials spoke English. Castletown was the capital of the island and the place of the lord's residence, finally being displaced in favour of Douglas only in 1869.

During the 17th century conditions started to change rather radically as 'the running trade' – smug-

Old railway viaduct in Glen Mooar

gling – took hold. Man's strategic position, helped by its low custom duties, made it ideal for this form of activity which grew to such proportions that by the 18th century it became necessary for the British government to 'take control' by introducing the Revesting and Mischief acts in 1765. These effectively meant that sovereignty of the island was once more vested in the Crown, and smuggling was curtailed.

The 'Revestment' was a humiliation and an economic disaster for the Manx people, for although Tynwald still remained, it could pass no laws costing money because the customs duties were diverted to the British government. This situation continued until 1866, when the Manx customs revenue was transferred back to the island's revenue, but with the stipulation that ultimate control over spending should rest with the British Treasury. This situation was only repealed in 1958, since when the island has had the freedom to conduct its own affairs.

Looking forward to Niarbyl from Lhiattee ny Beinnee

GEOLOGY AND VEGETATION

The bulky upland mass of the island is a much-mangled thrust of old slaty rocks, known as the Manx slate series, and consisting of clay slates, grits and greywackes, probably Ordovician, rather like the Skiddaw slates of the English Lake District, which also re-appear in the south-west of that region. The slates were refolded several times during the Caledonian mountain-building period and outcrop now in the axis of the island. During this time, the rock mass was penetrated by molten material that formed dykes, most noticeable along the coast, where the slates or grits are exposed.

During Carboniferous times the sandstones that proliferate around Castletown and Port St Mary were laid down. Near Peel, a distinctive red sandstone provides an easily workable material for building stone and appears, along with Castletown limestone, in many buildings on the island.

Solid rocks at surface level are rare, though Carboniferous, Permian and Triassic deposits lie beneath the lowlands at the northern end of the island, covered by glacial drift to a depth of 50m (164ft) or more.

Three successive glacial periods are thought to have affected the island, with glacial deposits most noticeable in the north, but still significant elsewhere. The ice sheets came mainly from south-west Scotland and north-east Ireland, and boulder clays, along with sands and gravels, are distributed over much of the island.

An unusual feature of the Manx landscape, something that has existed for centuries, is the almost complete absence of trees. It is clear that when humans first arrived, the coastal lands would have been covered in oak woods, but today trees only occur in the sheltered glens and recent re-afforestation areas.

FLORA AND FAUNA

The immense diversity of habitat on the Isle of Man generates a range of flora and fauna bordering on the spectacular. There are wild flowers throughout the year, from the primroses, celandine, sorrel and wood anemone of spring, when the rafts of wild garlic are already filling the air with their pungent smell and bluebells are starting to carpet whatever

remaining stands of woodland they can find. Gorse is already in heady scented bloom come early April, when the delicate coastal squill, sea campion and thrift are also starting to flower. Orchids flourish in June, while the heathers that bring a purple hue to the Manx hillsides start to flower from July onwards. Later in the year, into autumn, a few sheltered woodland spots start to produce fungi as the great colour change of the year begins. Throughout the year it is impossible not to notice the luxuriant growth of lichens, mosses and liverworts – clear indicators of a clean and healthy climate.

The island is well suited to birdlife and a free leaflet from tourist information centres tells you where to look, and when, for the island's most interesting species. These include

Cattle, Port Grenaugh

In Glen Trunk

red-throated, black-throated and great northern divers, Manx shearwater, storm petrel, water rail, hen harrier, bar-tailed godwit, long- and short-eared owls, siskin, redpoll, crossbill and chough.

CLIMATE

Because of the influence of the Irish Sea, the Manx climate is temperate and lacking in extremes. In winter, snowfall and frost are infrequent. On the rare occasions that snow does occur, it rarely lies for more than a day or two. February tends to be the coldest month, with an average daily temperature of 4.9°C (41°F), but it is also often dry. However, the island is rather windy. The prevailing wind direction for most of the island is

from the south-west, although the complex topography means that local effects of shelter and exposure are very variable. In summer, April, May and June are the driest months, while May, June and July are the sunniest. July and August are the warmest months, with an average daily maximum temperature around 17.6°C (63°F). The highest temperature recorded at the island's weather centre at Ronaldsway is 28.9°C or 84°F. Thunderstorms are rare.

Although geographically small, there is, nevertheless, significant climatic variation around the island. Sea fog affects the south and east coasts at times, especially in spring, but is less frequent in the west. Rainfall and the frequency of hill fog both increase with altitude. The highest point of the island – Snaefell at 621m (2036ft) – receives some 2¼ times more rainfall than Ronaldsway on the south-east coast, where the annual average is 863mm (34ins).

THE THREE LEGS OF MAN

No one really knows how the Three Legs of Man motif, the symbol of independence, came to be adopted as the national emblem of the Isle of Man. The three-legged device certainly has a long history, dating far back into pagan times and represents the sun and its daily passage across the heavens. The Manx form was derived from a design that showed the spokes of a wheel and which, in turn, represented the rays of the sun. This has led to it being described as a solar wheel, a symbol of pagan sun worship. Other related symbols include the cross and the fylfot, or four-legged swastika.

It is believed that Alexander III of Scotland may have adopted it when he gained control of the Isle of Man following the defeat of King Haakon of Norway at Largs in 1263 and the end of Norse rule that followed. Credence is given to this notion by the fact that the seal of King Harald Olaffson, granting a mining charter to the monks of Furness Abbey in 1246, still bore a ship emblem as its seal, not the Three Legs motif. The oldest representation of the Three Legs in existence is on the Manx Sword of State, and there is another use on the Maughold Market Cross now in St Maughold's Church.

Coastline, Langness

GETTING THERE

By air

The island is primarily serviced by British Airways CitiExpress and British European flying various routes to Ronaldsway Airport. Frequent flights are provided to and from London (Gatwick, London City and Luton), Manchester, Liverpool, Bristol, Blackpool, Birmingham, Glasgow, Leeds/Bradford, Jersey and Dublin. There are also daily connecting flights linking the island to Newcastle, Edinburgh, East Midlands and Southampton and to many international destinations. Overall, the Isle of Man Airport is the 22nd busiest in the British Isles in terms of passengers handled.

On arrival on the island, you are greeted with a very modern airport terminal, recently refurbished and extended. The terminal has an assortment of shops, café, seating areas and telephones. Security checks exist as in all UK national airports. In addition, flights to and from Ireland are subject to duty free allowances.

Getting through the airport is relatively quick compared to UK airports. Immediately outside the airport terminal is the main bus route and stop for travelling to Douglas and the south. Inside the terminal are a number of car hire firms.

By sea

The island's principal port is Douglas, which has deep-water berths and facilities for handling passengers, cars and freight vehicles and general cargoes. Peel, on the west coast, has

Glen Maye coastline

16

a deep-water berth and facilities for handling limited passenger traffic and general cargoes. Ramsey in the north-east is a drying harbour with a busy trade in general and bulk cargoes.

The island's main sea routes are between Douglas and Liverpool, and Douglas and Heysham, a modern port in the north-west of England closely linked to Britain's motorway and intercity rail networks. The Isle of Man Steam Packet Company operates multi-purpose and freight RORO vessels on the Heysham route providing twice-daily services throughout the year for passengers, cars and freight vehicles. The Steam Packet Company also has twice-daily fast craft services to Liverpool from April to October and conventional weekend services during the winter.

In the summer months the Steam Packet operates additional fast craft routes for holiday traffic to Dublin and Belfast as well as extra sailings to Heysham and Liverpool with SeaCat and SuperSeaCat fast craft.

GETTING ABOUT

By car or motor bike

All vehicles must be insured and you should have your driving licence with you. Although not mandatory, it's advisable to have breakdown vehicle cover, first aid kit, warning triangle and fire extinguisher.

Douglas is the busiest place on the island and best avoided around 8–9am and 5–6.30pm when the business traffic is at its heaviest. Parking in Douglas and some town areas can be a problem. 'Pay and Display' parking is prevalent, as are yellow lines. Free disc parking is available in towns and villages – discs, available free from shops, car hire companies and on board ferries, must be set to show time of arrival on the dashboard. Disc parking zones, which are clearly signed, range from 15 minutes to two hours.

Driving around the island is generally relaxed and enjoyable. Typical A and B roads, together with country lanes prevail. Speed limits vary across the island, and the best advice is to stay below 30mph in built-up areas and 50mph elsewhere.

It is an offence to use a hand-held mobile phone while driving your car, punishable with a fine of up to £1000.

Steam train

Running in the summer season (Easter to September) from Douglas to Port Erin, the steam train takes about 1 hour 10 minutes for the journey, with several stations to stop off on the way. Tickets are available from the main stations. Douglas Station is about 10 minutes' walk from the Sea Terminal.

Horse tram

The horse-drawn trams complete a circuit along Douglas promenade from outside the Sea Terminal to Derby Castle at the opposite end of the promenade. These operate during

17

Port Cornaa

the summer season only. Travel time is approximately 30 minutes each way. Tickets can be purchased on board.

Electric train

The Manx Electric Railway operates all year round, except Christmas week, from Douglas promenade (Derby Castle) all the way to Laxey. You then have a choice to continue to Ramsey or (summer only) take the alternative route up Snaefell.

The time to Laxey is about 30 minutes. From there to Ramsey is about the same, and the trip to the summit of Snaefell likewise.

Bus

A national bus service operates throughout the island connecting all the towns, villages and district areas.

The frequency of the different services depends very much on the nature of the destination and the departure points. Prices are relatively cheap and multi-day passes can be purchased. Isle of Man resident OAPs travel for free – but there are no concessions for visiting pensioners.

Taxi

There are taxi ranks and car hire firms all over the island.

Car hire

Hire cars are available at the Sea Terminal, the airport terminal, delivered to your hotel or picked up at certain garages. Booking is advised. You will need to be 21 or over, have a valid driving licence and possibly your passport.

ACCOMMODATION

There is a wide range of excellent accommodation from prime hotels to inexpensive B&Bs right across the island, though there are no hostels as such. All the walks in this book were completed from bases at Orrisdale (Kirk Michael) and Colby Glen, but the island's road and public transport network is such that it matters not which town or village is used.

WALKING THE ISLAND

The scope for walking on the island is considerable, and with a very distinctive flavour. Being an island, and a smallish one at that, many walks touch upon the coastline at some point, and it is probably true to say that on every walk in this book you can see the sea at some stage.

There is limited opportunity for great long walks, though the diligent person can string together quite a few of these walks to make something more demanding. But the emphasis here is on shorter walks, suitable for half days, or for families. More committed walkers will still find they can spend long days crossing the hills that form the central spine of the island, but the total number of opportunities to do so are limited. Even so, you can come here for a month and still follow a new walk every day.

And being so close to the sea produces its own brand of weather conditions for the walker to contend with – from hot balmy days to real howlers on the tops. Sea mist can be quite a problem, too, so if you can't navigate in poor visibility, it would be a good idea to wait for a clear day.

Rounding Maughold

Unlike parts of the UK, great swathes of the Isle of Man are areas known as 'Public Ramblage'. In essence this means there is a freedom to roam at will. Large parts of the high ground fall within this definition, making the Isle of Man significantly ahead of the UK in this as well as in other things. Other areas hold 'Scenic Significance' or are held by the Manx National Trust or Manx National Heritage, and here access is generally not a problem, though there may be local restrictions. Elsewhere, the island has 17 National Glens, maintained and preserved by the Forestry Department because it is largely in the glens that the island's main areas of tree cover are to be found. There are two types of glen, coastal and mountain. The coastal glens – like Glen Maye, Groudle Glen, Glen Wyllin and Dhoon Glen – often lead down to a beach, while the mountain glens – Sulby, Glen Mooar, Colby Glen – have splendid streams, waterfalls and pools.

One of the problems, probably the only significant problem, for walkers visiting the island was the mapping. The British Ordnance Survey produce a single Landranger map (Sheet 95), at a scale of 1:50,000, and experienced walkers will find this adequate. But, at the time of writing, there was no corresponding larger scale OS map, either Pathfinder or Explorer. What exisited was a two-sheet 1:25,000 Outdoor Leisure Map produced by the Isle of Man by reducing old six-inch maps. The result was often text too small to read with the naked eye, although rights of way were clearly depicted. A modern 1:30,000 map, produced by Harvey Maps, became available in the spring of 2004. The Isle of Man maps are available at shops across the island.

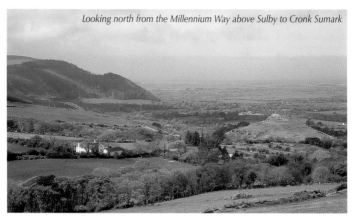

Looking north from the Millennium Way above Sulby to Cronk Sumark

WALK 1

Ayres, Point of Ayre and Bride

Distance:	12km (7½ miles)
Map:	Isle of Man Outdoor Leisure Map: North
Start/Finish:	Ayres Visitor Centre (grid ref 435038)
Parking:	At start
Refreshments:	Green Parrot Tea Room in Bride

This walk is essentially for those people who love the sea and for birdwatchers. The coastline here plays host to almost every species of bird listed on the island at some time during each year, including some interesting migratory, passage birds. Unfortunately there is quite a bit of road walking to make the walk into a proper circuit, and this detracts from the walk a little as well as introducing a note of danger as the roads have no verges – the area near the Ayres lighthouse is used as a refuse dump (albeit extremely well controlled) and as a base for crushing stone, so there are quite a lot of heavy vehicles to contend with. Consider retracing your steps rather than doing the road section, or make a start at Bride instead: there is a large car park there.

Point of Ayre lighthouse

21

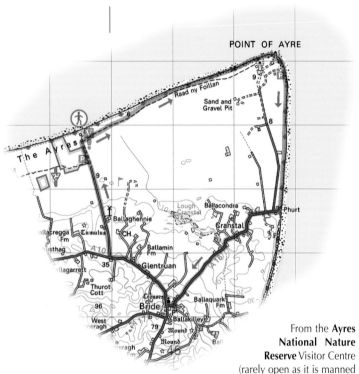

From the **Ayres National Nature Reserve** Visitor Centre (rarely open as it is manned by volunteers), walk back along the access road for about 50m to a paved path heading towards the distant lighthouse. When the paving ends, the path continues as a broad grassy track, running close enough to the upper level of the beach to give good sightings of the birdlife here. My most recent visit produced ringed plover, little tern, common/arctic tern, oystercatcher, curlew, black-throated diver, eider, shag, cormorant, gannet, stonechat, meadow pipit and skylark. This is a favoured breeding ground for birds, so during the breeding season care needs to be exercised in the placement of one's feet, and any dogs need the control of a tight rein.

Ayres National Nature Reserve

The nature reserve has a total area of 272ha (673 acres). The site is internationally important for breeding birds, and the whole area outstanding for natural historians. Out at sea gannet, shag, cormorant, guillemot, and little, common and arctic terns are frequent visitors – along with the occasional black-throated and great northern diver. Don't be surprised to spot the dorsal fins of whales and porpoises, as well as the bobbing heads of grey seals. Along the shore, and inland among the dunes and heath, expect to find ringed plover, oystercatcher, sanderling, dunlin, curlew, stonechat, skylark and whinchat. Wild flowers are especially rich here, and include pyramidal and early purple orchids, wild thyme and burnet rose. From 1 May to 31 July, dogs must be on a lead.

Fishermen favour this northernmost tip of the island, and can often be seen here, shore casting for mackerel or plaice.

Just having passed the **lighthouse**, you either bear right or get your feet wet, as the coastline heads south. Offshore it is not unusual to be treated to the sight of some turbulent water: two different tidal systems meet here and can produce quite a frenzy on a good day. But on dry land, the route heads south, now following a route that passes a domestic refuse site, and continues just above the shore edge as far as a couple of cottages at Phurt. You can turn inland a little earlier than this, when the ongoing track does so, but otherwise you are left with a narrow, field-edge path to take you on to Phurt.

From here on, all is road walking. First to the lovely village of Bride, with its church dedicated to St Bridget. And from there through Glen Truan as far as the turning to Ballaghennie Farm, a road lovely in spring with wild flowers, that leads down to the shore.

Ayres lighthouse

The Point of Ayre lighthouse, controlled by the Northern Lights Board of Scotland, not Trinity House, as might be supposed, was built between 1815 and 1818 by Robert Stevenson, the grandfather of Robert Louis Stevenson.

WALK 2

Maughold, Port Mooar and Port e Vullen

Distance:	7km (4⅓ miles)
Map:	Isle of Man Outdoor Leisure Map: North
Start/Finish:	Maughold (grid ref 495917)
Parking:	Maughold Head

There are many places where the Manx coastal scenery is outstanding; north of the small village of Maughold (pronounce it Mackle't and you'll be close), it is exceptional. This walk first visits the lovely bay of Port Mooar before racing by road to Port e Vullen and making a lazy return along part of the Raad ny Foillan.

The starting point is difficult to find; it's along a concealed road that branches from the very entrance of **St Maughold's Church**. The road eventually leads to Maughold lighthouse, but before getting there, keep an eye open for a narrow, branching track on the left (shortly after turning away from the

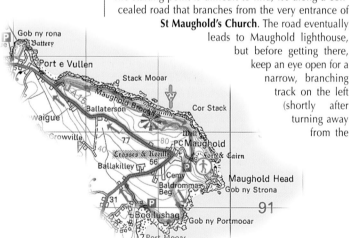

St Maughold's Church

churchyard), with a footpath sign at its foot. This leads up to a large parking area from where you can make an optional descent to visit St Maughold's Well – the path down is quite steep and care is needed in wet weather.

From the car park go back down the lane and turn right towards the churchyard, wherein there is a fine collection of Manx cross slabs and, in the church, one of the earliest examples of the Triskellion, the Manx three legs emblem.

Kirk Maughold Cross-house

Located within the churchyard of St Maughold's, the cross-house contains the island's largest display of cross slabs, dating from the 7th century. At first glance, these are simply a collection of weathered and faded crosses housed in a shelter open to the elements. But closer inspection reveals a treasury of Celtic and Manx history, with good and clear examples of runic inscriptions. The Manx crosses are a study in themselves, and it is fitting to find so many together. Almost one-third of the pre-Norse crosses found on the island are preserved here.

St Maughold and the parish church

Maughold was a native of Ulster, and by all accounts not the most Christian-living of people, having been found guilty of murder. He was brought before St Patrick, who felt unable to absolve him of his sins, and ordered that it be left in the hands of God by casting the luckless soul adrift in a coracle. With God's good grace shining upon him, Maughold eventually reached the Isle of Man where he met two men who taught him the word of God with such evident success that Maughold succeeded them as bishop. In a slight variation on this theme, St Maughold is acclaimed as the person who first brought Christianity to the island.

The parish church at Maughold, and its graveyard, form a centre of religious significance that is unique in the Isle of Man. The church itself is not dissimilar to other Manx churches, but the churchyard, which was the site of Maughold's Celtic monastery dating from the 7th century, contains numerous reminders of the island's Celtic and Viking past, from the oblong forms of three ancient *keeills* (chapels) to the largest single collection of cross slabs anywhere. The churchyard also contains the graves of many notable Manx people, from William Callister, founder of the Isle of Man Bank and Robert Faragher, a radical champion of the campaign to secure the popular election of the House of Keys, to the Hall Caine Monument, a memorial to the successful Manx novelist.

Within the church will be found the Maughold parish cross, a weathered work of art made from sandstone brought from the Cumbrian coast at St Bees, depicting one of the earliest forms of the Three Legs of Man. It dates from the 14th century, and is the only remaining such cross on the island. The workmanship, in spite of hundreds of years of weathering is still discernibly remarkable.

Built on the site of an earlier structure, the church of St Maughold may well have been the seat of the Manx bishopric. The present church retains nothing that pre-dates the 11th century (the Irish Romanesque arch of the west doorway is thought to date from this time), though there are some lovely 13th-century windows in the south walls of the nave.

At the churchyard wall, take the lane going left and down through a gate. The ongoing track wanders down through hedgerows, embankments and low stone walls. Eventually, the track reaches a couple of gates giving into fields. Go over a stile beside the left-hand one of these, and keep forward down the ensuing field to a ladder-stile at the bottom. Over this go left down to the seashore, where Maughold lighthouse comes into view, and turn right along a delightful shoreline path, which pursues a splendid line just above the water's edge and eventually turns into the bay of Port Mooar. Go towards a white shore cottage and, immediately after it, turn right up a lane, climbing to a T-junction. Turn right and walk up to the village of Maughold.

At this point the walk can be shortened by turning along the track around the churchyard and following it back to the car park.

Otherwise, turn left out of the village, following the road for about 1.6km (1 mile), as far as a signposted enclosed path on the right to **Maughold Brooghs**. Along this stretch of road there are fine views left to the ridge of North Barrule and Clagh Ouyr, beyond which the summit of Snaefell can also be picked out.

Maughold Brooghs
The coastline of Maughold is very steep, and much-favoured by breeding birds. Here is the island's largest colony of cormorants, along with substantial numbers of kittiwake, guillemot, black guillemot, puffin, peregrine falcon, chough and raven. Out at sea, don't be surprised to see the bobbing head of a grey seal from time to time, or a basking shark, which are known to frequent these waters.

At a gate, enter the Manx National Trust property going forward on a fine grassy path high above the inlet of Port e Vullen. As in many places on the island, the path is flanked by healthy stands of gorse, which bring vivid colour to the day along with their heady aroma like cinnamon and coconut.

The path steadily works a way around the headland and climbs to a double shelter and topograph from which the southern coast of Scotland and the fells of the Lake District are visible. From the topograph, continue with the clear path and eventually you will return to the car park above St Maughold's Well.

WALK 3
Cornaa, Glen Mona and Ballaglass Glen

Distance:	7km (4½ miles)
Map:	Isle of Man Outdoor Leisure Map: North
Start/Finish:	Cornaa (grid ref 466899)
Parking:	Entrance to Ballaglass Glen
Refreshments:	Glen Mona Hotel

Between Port Mooar, near Maughold, and Laxey, the Raad ny Foillan spends most of its time inland of the coast, only once touching on it, and that all-too-briefly at the lovely Port Cornaa. The walk down Glen Cornaa is truly beautiful and terminates at a neat cove from where one Swedish entrepreneur had planned to export gunpowder. Alas, he failed to discuss his manufacturing plans with the Manx government, which adopted a fairly forceful attitude to the oversight.

The bay at Port Cornaa

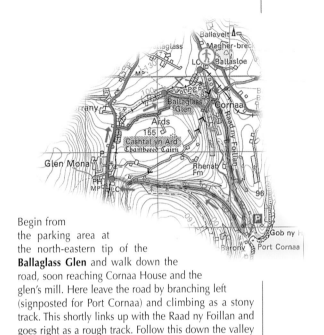

Begin from the parking area at the north-eastern tip of the **Ballaglass Glen** and walk down the road, soon reaching Cornaa House and the glen's mill. Here leave the road by branching left (signposted for Port Cornaa) and climbing as a stony track. This shortly links up with the Raad ny Foillan and goes right as a rough track. Follow this down the valley into mature woodland of beech and oak.

Ballaglass Glen

The 6.4ha (16 acres) of Ballaglass Glen were acquired in 1952 by the Manx government, and the area is now managed as semi-natural woodland. The tree species consist of mature oak with beech, larch and pine, and some natural regeneration of willow, birch and ash around old mine buildings. Ballaglass Glen was once the home of an important corn mill, last used in 1951. It was a typical Manx mill with threshing facilities and drying kiln in addition to the grinding machinery. The stone buildings found in the glen were erected by the Great Mona Mining Company, which operated from 1854 until 1857 and again from 1866 to 1867 mining a vein of zinc and copper. The mine was short-lived, but typical of the many mines of the days of speculative mining in the 19th century.

Eventually the track descends to a gate giving into riverside pasture. Here keep forward, heading for the cove ahead. A new bridge has been constructed over the river on the right (at the time of writing it is unclear whether this is intended for public use, as the track on the other side leading down to Port Cornaa is not a right of way). Ignore this bridge, and keep away from the river, eventually being steered by a fence to a small footbridge near a beach cottage. Cross the bridge and go left to the pebbly beach, a lovely secluded spot.

Now walk up the road that leads away from the beech. There is lovely woodland on the glenside, and though paths seem to run through it, they are not rights of way. Fortunately, the road is generally quiet: mosses and wood sorrel grow on top of the walls, birds fill the hedgerows with song and the heady scent of wild ransomes lies heavily on the air.

Follow the road until another appears from the right, at a ford. Here cross a nearby footbridge and go forward onto a signposted path for Glen Mona. The track is initially stony, climbing beside a stream and then between steep embankments before wandering on agreeably through a narrow wooded glen.

The track climbs to meet and cross the Manx Electric Railway (take care here, and listen for trams). Continue in the same direction up to reach the main Laxey–Ramsey road, opposite the Glen Mona Hotel.

Turn right and walk along the roadside footpath for about 800m until you can leave it at a cottage called Hill Crest by turning right onto a signposted track, soon crossing the railway again, this time by a bridge. A lovely, gorsey track now ensues, taking the route through a few twists and turns. When it forks at a footpath signpost, keep left, and keep following the main thrust of the track which finally reaches the edge of Ballaglass Glen.

Cross the immediate track and go down steps to emerge at the Ballaglass Glen Railway Station. Turn immediately right here to re-enter the glen. Go down steps to a footbridge spanning the glen river. When the path forks, near an old building, bear right.

The path shortly descends to run above the glen's river again, but, just after you pass a riverside picnic area, climb to the left, away from the river, to intercept another track, descending to the right. Turn onto this and follow it downriver to emerge on the Port Cornaa road at Cornaa House and the old mill. Turn left here and walk back up the road to the parking area and starting point.

Track leading through Glen Mona

WALK 4

Clagh Ouyr and North Barrule

Distance:	9.5km (6 miles)
Map:	Isle of Man Outdoor Leisure Map: North
Start/Finish:	Black Hut (grid ref 406885)
Parking:	Black Hut

North Barrule, dominating the northern coastal town of Ramsey, is the second-highest hill on the island and its shapely summit is a distinctive feature. There is a steep and rugged ascent from The Hibernian, near Ramsey, but a much less strenuous ascent can be made from the Black Hut, below Snaefell, high on the TT Course. The going can be soft underfoot, but only in patches, and the return dips into the Cornaa Valley.

North Barrule from Maughold

Cross the road with care, at all times of the year there are motorcyclists and motorists who like to test their skills and your nerves on this upland part of the TT Course. Go over a step-stile beside a gate, descending a little before climbing to a signpost at a wall corner. From the signpost strike upwards

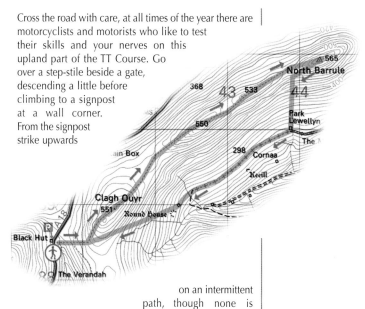

on an intermittent path, though none is needed, gradually bearing left as the ridge is approached and pulling easily onto the first top, Clagh Ouyr.

North Barrule now lies 4km (2½ miles) away, with the route lying across two minor, unnamed summits on the way. In places the terrain is boggy, but this can be avoided in all but the worst weather.

As you approach North Barrule, a wall stands before the final steepish pull to the summit, which is a stunning viewpoint embracing the whole of the northern part of the island, and, on the distant horizons, the fells of the English Lake District and the mountains of Galloway.

Retrace your steps to the wall and there turn left, descending the southern flank of the mountain into the Cornaa Valley, aiming for the ruins of Park Llewellyn Farm.

At the ruins, turn right on a broad track heading up the valley, keeping an eye open for the walled St Mary's Church (Keeil Noo Voirrey) on the left.

Continue heading up the valley, steadily rising now, to a small building and sheep enclosures. Clagh Ouyr is now ahead and slightly to the right as the track dwindles to a path and then peters out altogether. Climbing more steeply now, aim to the south of Clagh Ouyr, to avoid needless ascent. Strong walkers can more or less head upwards to meet the outward route, but otherwise a course around the southern end of the hill will be easier to maintain.

Once back on the ridge and the line of the outward route is rejoined, it is simply a matter of heading downhill in the direction of the Black Hut. A final, uphill pull leads to the road and the end of the walk.

Clagh Ouyr from Mountain Hut

WALK 5
Snaefell from the Bungalow

Distance:	6.7km (4 miles)
Map:	Isle of Man Outdoor Leisure Map: North
Start/Finish:	Bungalow (grid ref 396868)
Parking:	Bungalow
Refreshments:	Summit (seasonal)

The highest part of a country has always drawn attention, for a variety of reasons, not all of them good. The top of Snaefell is no exception, and the desire of Victorians to look down on the island led to the building of the Snaefell Mountain Railway to transport them to the top without undue fatigue. Modern communications have also imposed a tariff, cluttering the summit with man-made paraphernalia. Sadly, it is the ability to ride to the summit and have a cup of tea that makes Snaefell interesting, for without these trappings this would simply be another fundamentally uninteresting hill, the highest of five Marilyns on the island.

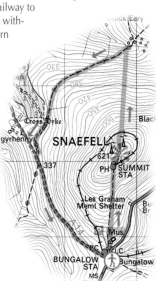

Just beyond the road junction and **mountain railway** crossing point high on the Ramsey to Douglas road, a gate on the left gives onto a steadily rising footpath that leads unerringly to the summit café less than a mile distant. Keep to the right of the building to locate a concrete walkway heading towards a radio mast, and leave this when convenient to walk across to the summit trig and topograph.

Snaefell Mountain Railway

The Snaefell Mountain Railway celebrated its centenary in 1995, and it still operates with its six original tramcars, the only electric mountain railway in the British Isles. With gradients as steep as 1 in 12 in places, there is a central 'Fell' rail which helps the cars to break. It is 8.8km (5½ miles) from base to summit and construction of the 3ft 6in (107cm) gauge track was begun in January 1895. Barely seven months later, on 21 August 1895, it opened to the public. Today the line operates from the end of April to late September.

Walkers who do not want to experience the rigours of the tussock moorland to the north of the summit, should simply retreat the way they came.

Otherwise, set off from the summit roughly following grid north, targeting a small plantation at grid ref 396902. The terrain is untracked but generally easy if occasionally wet, and populated by a few moorland birds – meadow pipit, grouse and curlew – as well as mountain hare. Hen harriers, peregrine, long- and short-eared owls also feature here.

The objective is to locate a signpost for the Millennium Way near the top of the valley leading north-west to the Block Eary Reservoir. Once this has been found, turn left on an indistinct trod across the moorland, indistinct but improving after a while, once the next signpost has been reached. Thereafter it scampers agreeably across the north-west shoulder of Snaefell, reaching the Sulby Glen road a little under 1.6km (1 mile) from the Bungalow. Turn left and follow the roadside verge back to the start.

WALK 6
Laxey, Agneash and King Orry's Grave

Distance:	6.5km (4 miles)
Map:	Isle of Man Outdoor Leisure Map: North
Start/Finish:	Laxey (grid ref 433847)
Parking:	Laxey

It will take a short diversion from this route to visit the famous Laxey waterwheel, but it is well worth the effort just to see this remaining monument to Manx mining industry. Otherwise, the route wanders up to the lovely white-cottaged village of Agneash before looping across country to connect with the coastal path and a visit to King Orry's Grave.

Begin from the car park along the Laxey Wheel road and walk up the road, passing the tourist information centre and then branching right on a descending lane that passes the fire station and continues alongside the Mooar River prior to returning to the road.

Maintain the same direction, soon crossing a road bridge spanning the river, just after which footpaths climb to the **Laxey Wheel**. Having visited the wheel, return to the same point, and turn up the road to Agneash.

Walk all the way up to Agneash and there, as the road bends left, leave it by branching

37

The Laxey Wheel

Famed afar as the largest waterwheel in the world, the Laxey Wheel, the Lady Isabella (named after the then Governor's wife) was built in 1854, at a time when the Manx mining industry was in its heyday. The purpose of the wheel was to pump water from the lead mines. It has a circumference of 84m (276ft), a diameter of 23m (75ft), and is capable of lifting 1140 litres (251 gallons) of water per minute from mines more than 330m (1083ft) deep. The Laxey mines were originally opened in 1750 and were entered from surface adits rather than shafts. They were enormously productive and proved a steady investment. By the 1850s an initial £80 share had risen in value to over £1000, an impressive return for a lead mine by the standards of the day.

King Orry's Grave

right, near a cottage called The Orchids, onto a sign-posted footpath descending some steps and then becoming enclosed as it heads for the Glen Agneash burn, crossed by a wooden footbridge, with more steps beyond it.

At the top of the steps, turn right on a grassy footpath to a gate, and follow the ensuing path as it rises gently through gorse and climbs past a ruined building. There's a fine view backwards at this point, over the village of Agneash, set against a fine backdrop of the Laxey Glen and Snaefell.

The path climbs to a metal kissing-gate and from there goes forward as a broad grassy track across the centre of a sloping pasture to a gate in the top corner. Over a stile beside the gate, bear right alongside a fence to a step-stile giving onto a gorse-enclosed footpath, which leads up to pass behind a row of cottages. From the rear corner, keep left onto a narrow grassy path heading for a distant farm building, which leads to a ladder-stile giving onto a broad track bearing right, through a small plantation.

Keep following the track to a T-junction, turn right and, 30m later, go left through a gate and onto a broad enclosed track that leads up to a farm. A step-stile crosses a fence, beyond which a path runs behind farm buildings to a metal gate giving out onto a farm lane. Turn left and walk out to a T-junction.

The countryside here, undulating, patterned by gorse hedgerows, is especially beautiful and much favoured by patrolling hen harriers, kestrels and short-eared owls.

King Orry's Grave

These are the remains of a prehistoric chambered tomb, built and used by a community of farmers about 5000 years ago. The tomb, a long barrow of complex design, consisted of a line of stone-built chambers buried under a cairn of earth and stones. There were at least three chambers beyond the entrance and they were roofed with stone slabs and covered over to create the cairn. The chambers would have been filled with burials, starting with the furthest. When excavated, few remains had survived, save one small piece of earthenware similar to other pieces found at the Meayll circle near Cregneash. Access to the tomb would have taken place during commemorative ceremonies and the passage into the tomb and between the chambers would have been intentionally difficult to reinforce the division between the living world and the afterlife.

Today the site is in two parts, split by the road. If, as is supposed, the two halves are of the same tomb, then it was indeed both complex and large. For two centuries, a tradition persisted that the two parts were connected, but clear evidence has been obscured by the construction of the road and cottages. The grave was abandoned during the neolithic period and since then the blocks above the entrance have collapsed.

King Orry is a semi-legendary character revered by the Manx as their greatest king, Godred Crovan, who reigned from 1079 and created the kingdom of Mann and the Isles, stretching from the Irish Sea to the Outer Hebrides. Although numerous monuments are named in deference to him, there is no connection between the historical figure and these prehistoric remains. King Orry is believed to lie buried on the Scottish island of Islay.

At the T-junction, turn right and eventually emerge on a main road, shared by the coastal path. Turn right and follow the road for almost 2km (1 mile) until you reach the site of **King Orry's Grave**, a dissected site with the remnants of the grave on either side of the road, but well worth taking a few moments to visit.

Continue down the road until you reach a crossroads, and there turn right towards **Laxey**. After about 200m, leave the roadside footpath by turning left onto a steeply descending concrete path that leads to a crossing point on the Manx Electric Railway. Continue on the other side, now through a narrow neck of woodland, and walk down to a lane junction beside the valley river. Turn right, go forward past a bridge and keep on past a retirement home.

Laxey

Deriving its name from Laxa, the Norse for salmon river, Laxey, until the 18th century, was little more than a huddle of fishermen's cottages along the coast between Douglas and Ramsey. Once mineral deposits had been discovered, however, a new village was built higher up the glen, built largely to accommodate the 600 men who came to work the mines. By 1857, the mines here were the principal source of zinc in the British Isles and also produced a quantity of lead ore containing silver. Following a steady decline towards the end of the 19th century, the mines finally closed in 1929.

Beyond this, turn left crossing a footbridge and climbing on the other side to a lane. Turn right and walk up to the main road, crossing it with care to return to the starting point.

WALK 7
The Snaefell Mines

Distance:	9km (5½ miles)
Map:	Isle of Man Outdoor Leisure Map: North
Start/Finish:	Laxey (grid ref 434847)
Parking:	Laxey
Refreshments:	Laxey

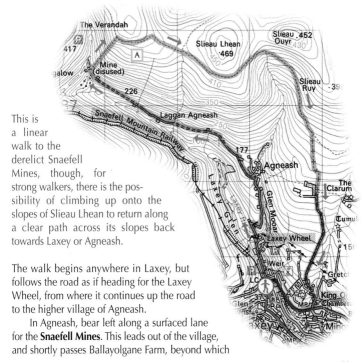

This is a linear walk to the derelict Snaefell Mines, though, for strong walkers, there is the possibility of climbing up onto the slopes of Slieau Lhean to return along a clear path across its slopes back towards Laxey or Agneash.

The walk begins anywhere in Laxey, but follows the road as if heading for the Laxey Wheel, from where it continues up the road to the higher village of Agneash.

In Agneash, bear left along a surfaced lane for the **Snaefell Mines**. This leads out of the village, and shortly passes Ballayolgane Farm, beyond which

41

Snaefell Mines

The Snaefell Mines were operated between 1856 and 1908, producing lead and zinc. Further attempts at extracting ore were made in the 1950s, but eventually the mine ceased operation. Inevitably with this type of mining, there was loss of life, the worst event occurring in May 1897, when 20 miners were lost.

the road surfacing ends and a rough track takes over. On the opposite side of the valley, the course of the Snaefell Mountain Railway can easily be picked out, carving a route up to the road crossing at the Bungalow.

There are a number of ruined cottages (*tholtans*) along the glen, which serve as a reminder of past times. Higher up the glen, the route crosses the inflowing Strooan ny Fasnee at a bridge, here entering an Area of Public Ramblage. About 800m further on, the track reaches the ruined buildings of the Snaefell Mines. If not climbing steeply onto the hillside to the north (Route A), simply retrace your outward route, and, if there's time, visit the Laxey Wheel.

Laxey Wheel

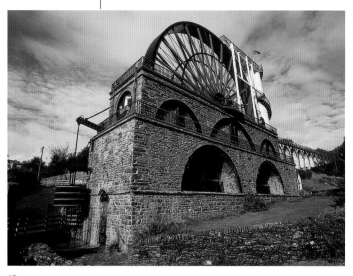

WALK 8
Sulby and the Millennium Way

Distance:	9.7km (6 miles)
Map:	Isle of Man Outdoor Leisure Map: North
Start/Finish:	Sulby Claddagh (grid ref 386940)
Parking:	Sulby Claddagh

This is an exhilarating walk, beginning beside the Sulby River and climbing high onto the gorse uplands to the south. Choose a clear day (the map, the signposting and the paths don't always agree and in poor visibility this could be a problem), and enjoy the airy freedom of mountain heath patrolled by hen harriers, kestrel and short-eared owls.

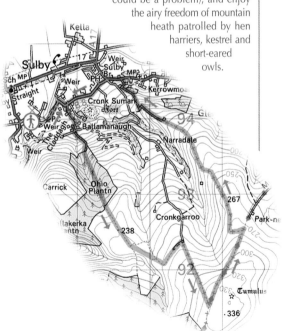

Striding out along the Millennium Way above Sulby

Set off alongside the Sulby River, going with the flow and parallel with a road, and when this bends right, go with it, soon to reach a bridge spanning an in-flowing burn. Ignore the bridge, and keep forward on a gently rising lane (signposted 'Snaefell Mountain Road'). Walk up the lane until the road surfacing ends and there branch left over a stile beside a gate, giving onto a rough track rising steadily to the edge of the Ohio Plantation.

Keep forward on a rising track that climbs to the top edge of the plantation and there leave it at a gate, going forward between gorse. The track is gated and eventually climbs to a convention of gates, a place where the right of way shown on the map and the tracks underfoot do not coincide.

Go forward, maintaining the same direction along a broad track with an earth embankment on the right. Continue up the track until a signpost directs the route left to a larger-than-normal ladder-stile. Over this, turn left again, along a broad grassy track, and keep going to a gate in a fence corner. From there, go forward on a rough track through heather that closes in on a wall on the left as it approaches two metal gates at the top of a rough road descending left to Sulby.

From the gates (ignore the road), turn right and strike up the heather moorland on a rutted track for just under 1km (⅔ mile). Keep going until the gradient levels as the track starts to swing towards the masted summit of Snaefell, and then look for a short branching track on the left, cutting through low heather to intercept the Millennium Way (though there is nothing immediate to confirm that it is the Millennium Way). Turn left, soon passing a right of way sign and, later, a low sign that does indeed confirm that you are on the Millennium Way.

Now gently descending, with a fine view north-wards across Sulby to the conspicuous white church at Jurby and the Ayres Nature Reserve, go as far as another gate at the head of a walled track. Here, without going through the gate, turn left alongside a wall to another gate giving onto a sunken track.

This track now leads all the way back to Sulby. Part way down it becomes partially surfaced, and is flanked throughout by gorse, stitchwort, violet, celandine, wild garlic, bluebell and intermittent stands of holly.

The track eventually descends to meet the main Sulby to Ramsey road. Take care emerging onto the road. Turn left and shortly go left again at the Ginger Hall Hotel. Turn left into River Meadow Land, following this back lane past the prehistoric site of Cronkshamerk (Cronk Sumark) hill fort (accessible by a steep climb from the roadside), after which you reach the road bridge encountered at the start of the walk. Cross it and turn right to follow the road back to the starting point.

WALK 9
Slieu Curn and Slieu Dhoo

Distance:	16.3km (10 miles)
Map:	Isle of Man Outdoor Leisure Map: North
Start/Finish:	Ballaugh (grid ref 348935)
Parking:	On-street parking (with care)
Refreshments:	Ballaugh and Sulby

In spite of its length, this walk is fairly straightforward and undemanding, but does offer the option of including Slieau Freoghane. There is also the possibility of visiting Killabrega, a deserted and ruinous farmstead high up on the western flank of Sulby Glen, though this will entail a longish amount of road walking to complete the route.

In Ballaugh go down the road past the One-Stop shop to a turning on the left onto the old railway line. Continue along the trackbed to the first main junction, at a gate, and here turn left and walk out to the main road.

At the road, turn left but, after about 100m, take the first turning on the right at Ballacob onto a side lane flanked by mature hedgerows. Follow the ascending lane and, when it forks, branch to the right. When the lane turns into Ballacurnkeil at the start of a green-way, the Bayr Glass, keep forward onto a dirt track between gorse hedgerows.

Follow the track, rising steadily onto the northern slopes of Slieu Curn. As the gradient eases, with Snaefell coming into view and, off to the right, the Mountains of Mourne in Northern Ireland and the hills of Galloway in Scotland. Continue to a gate and, through this, bear right on an ascending path onto open hillside.

Continue to a cattle grid and ladder-stile and then beyond continue along the greenway now with a spruce plantation (Slieu Curn Plantation) on the left. The track ascends steadily and then levels out at the head of Glen Dhoo, and keeps forward through a wall gap (old gate posts) with Snaefell in view on the left. Go on to a track junction where the track starts to climb again to meet a rough, stony track near a signpost. Here, turn onto the stony track, ignoring a branching green track on the left. Continue up the stony track, which gradually levels and then descends a little and runs on to a point below Slieu Freoghane.

Looking back to Slieu Curn from the slopes of Slieu Freoghane

Anyone wanting to bag Slieu Freoghane (one of five Marilyns on the island) should simply leave the track here and climb steeply to the summit on a clear, if boggy, path (Route C). The top is adorned by a large pole, trig pillar and quartz cairn. This will add about 1km (⅔ mile) to the distance, plus 100m (328ft) of ascent. Come back the same way to rejoin the broad stony track, which is heading south to Sartfell Plantation.

About 200m after the junction, between the main track and the extension to Slieu Freoghane, another clear, rutted track branches left, parallel with a wall and alongside a fence. Turn sharply onto this, still way-marked as a greenway, and follow it across the flanks of Slieau Dhoo.

The track eventually runs down to meet a gate, where the greenway ends. Keep forward with the ongoing track, which descends to meet a surfaced mountain road. Turn left. As the road later starts to bend to the left, leave it by branching right onto a stony track, once more the Bayr Glass.

Now again there is a choice. The main line (Route A) keeps forward across the western flank of Mount Karrin and eventually descends through Ballacuberagh Plantation to meet the Sulby Glen road. The alternative route (Route B), which visits Killabrega, immediately leaves the main route by branching right, heading towards Snaefell. The track descends to a five-bar

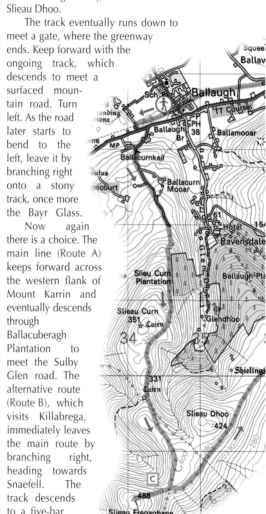

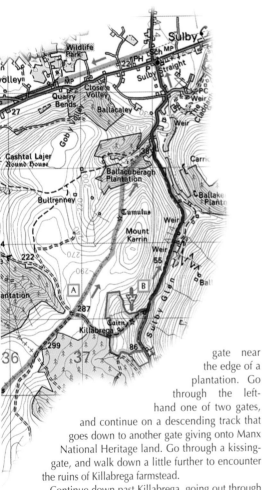

gate near
the edge of a
plantation. Go
through the left-
hand one of two gates,
and continue on a descending track that
goes down to another gate giving onto Manx
National Heritage land. Go through a kissing-
gate, and walk down a little further to encounter
the ruins of Killabrega farmstead.

Continue down past Killabrega, going out through
a wall gap, and then descending steeply towards the
Sulby Glen road below, roughly targeting a standing
stone in a roadside pasture on the other side of the valley

road. A path leads down through an expanse of bracken (seasonally overgrown) and reaches a fence corner where there is a small step-stile. Over this, continue along a steep, zig-zagging path down to the rear of a cottage. Here, bear right along an indistinct path that shortly turns down to reach the road.

On reaching the road, turn left and, taking care against approaching traffic, follow the valley road all the way to Sulby, passing the main line of the walk below Ballacuberagh Plantation.

In Sulby the continuation heads down the Jurby road, to the right of the Sulby Glen Hotel, until you once again encounter the old railway trackbed. Turn left onto this and keep on, passing the Curraghs Wildlife Park, to return to Ballaugh.

The ruins of Killabrega

WALK 10
Kirk Michael and Slieau Freoghane

Distance:	14km (8¾ miles)
Map:	Isle of Man Outdoor Leisure Map: North
Start/Finish:	Kirk Michael (grid ref 319909)
Parking:	Kirk Michael
Refreshments:	Kirk Michael

Slieau Freoghane – which Manx Gaelic speakers advise me is pronounced 'Sloo Ferrane' – is one of five Marilyns on the island, and likely to be popular on that count alone. But it is a fine hill to climb regardless of this dubious distinction, though the shortest and most direct route (for peak baggers only) is from the mountain road near Sartfell Plantation. This route partially reverses Walk 9, as far as Ballaugh, but then makes use of the old railway trackbed to return to Kirk Michael. It is a splendid walk, best reserved for a clear day, when the views over the western side of the island and across the Irish Sea to the mountains of Northern Ireland and northwards to southern Scotland are outstanding. There are times when the Mountains of Mourne seem so close you feel you could simply reach out and touch them.

There are a couple of car parks in Kirk Michael, but the key to the start of this walk is the lane opposite the turning into Glen Ballyre. Turn into this, a narrow lane that soon starts climbing, eventually deteriorating into a rough track that strikes up onto open moorland. High up on the hillside, having passed to the north of Slieau Freoghane, the track meets a huge cairn, Cairn Vael, largely the product of passing miners in years gone by, who would add another rock every time they walked by as a kind of talisman.

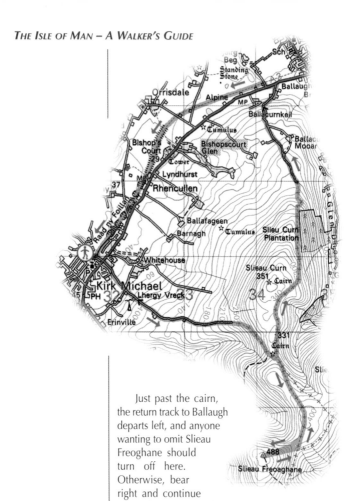

Just past the cairn, the return track to Ballaugh departs left, and anyone wanting to omit Slieau Freoghane should turn off here. Otherwise, bear right and continue along the stony track, ignoring a branching green track on the left. Gradually the track levels and then descends a little as it runs on to a point below Slieau Freoghane.

Now simply turn right and climb steeply to the top of Slieau Freoghane on a clear, if boggy, path. The top is adorned by a large pole, trig pillar and quartz cairn.

Retrace your ascent, and go left, back to the track junction near Cairn Vael, now keeping forward on a clear track heading for Slieau Curn and passing deeply defined Glen Dhoo on the right and Slieau Curn Plantation. The onward route is clear and not in doubt, leading eventually to an enclosed grassy track and then a surfaced lane (at Ballacurnkeil). Keep on, now following the surfaced lane, which leads down to the Kirk Michael – Ramsey road not far from Ballaugh.

Turn left for about 100m and take the first track on the right, which soon intercepts the course of the old railway. Turn left onto this and simply follow it for a little over 3.5km (2 miles) back to Kirk Michael.

Bishopscourt

WALK 11

Slieau Freoghane from the mountain road

Distance:	4km (2½ miles)
Map:	Isle of Man Outdoor Leisure Map: North
Start/Finish:	Sartfell Plantation (grid ref 342866)
Parking:	Parking area nearby
Refreshments:	Kirk Michael

This is a simple and direct way of 'bagging' Slieau Freoghane. The journey may be marginally extended by including the nearby Sartfell. The views are good, but other than that, this ascent has little to commend it other than directness – it's a peak bagger's route rather than a hill walker's.

From the mountain road go through the gate at the south-western corner of Sartfell Plantation onto a broad track that climbs at first alongside the plantation boundary. Shortly, having left the plantation behind, it bends around a stream as it passes onto the broad southern shoulder of Slieau Freoghane. At this point it is possible to bear left and walk easily up through the rough, heathery top of the hill on a variable path. Return by the same route.

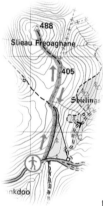

Walkers who want to make a longer day over this summit should consider ascending Slieau Freoghane from Kirk Michael (Walk 10), and from the top of the hill, cross through low heather to Sartfell, a

rounded lump. From the top of Sartfell, head north of west, down its broad shoulder, remaining within the Area of Public Ramblage to a gate at approximately grid ref 322876. Here the mountain road is reached. Turn right, down this to cross the TT Course and continue from Barregarrow to the branching track down towards Cooildarry Nature Reserve and Glen Wyllin. On meeting the Peel road, turn right to rejoin the TT Course at the edge of Kirk Michael.

Snaefell and Sulby Reservoir from the top of Slieau Freoghane

WALK 12

Glen Mooar

Distance:	3.2km (2 miles)
Map:	Isle of Man Outdoor Leisure Map: North
Start/Finish:	Glen Mooar (grid ref 303894)
Parking:	Glen Mooar Beach

The brief visit to one of the island's National Glens continues across the pasturelands of Michael parish, and makes a brief acquaintance with the Raad Ny Foillan.

From the car park, walk back up to the main road, and there cross to a gate opposite giving access to the **Glen Mooar National Glen**. Follow the main path through the glen, climbing steadily to reach a point directly above the Spooyt Vane waterfall. A detour to see the falls bears left along a permissive path.

Continue past the waterfall to a gate, beyond which turn right, ascending on a stony track, which climbs to a gate. Keep on to

Gorsey tracks above Glen Mooar

Remains of Patrick's Chapel in Glen Mooar woodlands

a second gate and continue climbing gently, now on a rutted vehicle track, as far as a signpost.

At the signpost turn right and pass through a gate onto a delightful gorse-banked track. The track leads down to a gate and shortly bears left, continuing to follow a well-defined route.

At the next signpost, at a junction of tracks, turn right and go through a gate and soon start descending past a farm. Bear right to walk out on its access track, following this until, at another signpost, it intercepts the Raad ny Foillan. Turn right onto this, walking for a short while until the trackbed that is its foundation comes to an end. Here turn left descending to rejoin Glen Mooar at the railway abutments encountered in the early part of the walk.

Turn left here and walk back out through the glen, retracing your outward route to the Glen Mooar Beach car park.

Glen Mooar National Glen

The glen extends from the main Peel to Kirk Michael road southwards to a small coniferous plantation beyond Spooyt Vane waterfall. In the central part of the glen lie the remains of Cabbal Pherick (Patrick's Chapel), an early Christian chapel dating from the 8th–10th century, now little more than a low-lying outline of the *keeill* (chapel) and surrounding burial ground and the remains of a priest's cell.

WALK 13
Orrisdale and Glen Trunk

Distance:	3.6km (2¼ miles)
Map:	Isle of Man Outdoor Leisure Map: North
Start/Finish:	Orrisdale (grid ref 327929)
Parking:	Limited roadside parking at Orrisdale

This deceptively simple walk is full of interest and has the advantage of seclusion. It wanders quiet lanes, visits the beach and comes back past one of the great seats of power on the island in times gone by.

The first part of the walk heads down the lane through the scattered hamlet of Orrisdale. Just before the Methodist chapel, a lane branches right at an interesting house with a weather vane and pump. This lane leads to a spot marked on the map as a cairn circle. Also known as the Druid's Circle on Cronk Koir, this is a pre-Christian site comprising large quartz boulders set in a circle.

Back on the village lane, go past the chapel and follow the lane through a few twists and turns as far as a signposted path branching on the right to the seashore. Beyond a gate a delightful grassy path leads down between gorse bushes towards the shore. This is Glen Trunk, quiet, secluded and little visited. The path leads past a **lime kiln** finally to reach a shoulder overlooking the beach just south of Orrisdale Head.

Lime kiln, Glen Trunk

Here, dip left to cross a wooden footbridge spanning the Glen Trunk burn, climbing on the other side to reach a vehicle access lane near an isolated cottage. Follow the lane out to meet a surfaced road. Go briefly left and then right into a field, following the field edge to a gate at the top of a narrow track, heading downhill until the old railway line that once operated along this stretch of coast is reached.

Turn left onto a footpath following the old trackbed, passing behind the impressive building, **Bishopscourt**. Go onward until the path finally emerges at a lane. Turn left, towards Orrisdale, to complete the walk.

Lime kiln

Just before reaching the seashore, there is a fine lime kiln tucked neatly into the flank of Glen Trunk. It is one of the largest and most complete to be found on the island. Although it isn't clear, it is likely that the lime would have been brought into the glen by boat and left on the shore for collection and processing.

Bishopscourt

One of the great houses of interest on the island, Bishopscourt's origins are traditionally attributed to Bishop Simon in the 13th century. It was a fortress tower and, in its early days, was moated – the old name for this and the surrounding area was Ballachurrey, which means 'marshy place'. The first mention of the building occurs in 1231, so there was evidently some significant building on this site before Bishop Simon arrived. In those days, the bishop was a vastly powerful man and, in his own right, a baron, with the power of life and death over his subjects, which gave this outpost something akin to the forts that developed throughout the Border Marches of Wales. Bishopscourt was sold into private hands in 1979, so ending more than seven centuries of association with the Diocese of Sodor and Man.

*Bluebell woodland
at Orrisdale*

WALK 14
A Taste of the Millennium Way

Distance:	11km (7 miles)
Map:	Isle of Man Outdoor Leisure Map: North
Start:	Bungalow (grid ref GR396868)
Finish:	Turning into Glen Auldyn (GR436943)
Transport:	You'll need to organise transport to either end, or use public transport
Refreshments:	Ramsey

This splendid walk is an unashamed excuse to wander along the Millennium Way and explore some of the wildest landscapes on the island. This is not a walk for misty days, when route-finding might be a problem in the early stages, but on a clear day there is an invigorating sensation about the austere moors, where hares dart about and moorland birds erupt dramatically ahead of you. The walk concludes with a visit to one of the most significant historic sites on the island – Sky Hill. The walk is linear, and walkers will therefore need to arrange transport to and from either end. It is possible, however, to use the Snaefell Mountain Railway from Laxey to reach the Bungalow, and to return by public transport to Ramsey and then by Manx Electric Railway (or buses) either to the start in Laxey or back to Douglas.

The Millennium Way is waymarked throughout, but in places the waymarks are well spaced out, making some of the sections potentially confusing to follow. For some, this will add to the pleasure of the walk, especially as it moves further away from Snaefell. Walkers who are happy wandering across trackless moorland could follow Walk 5 to the summit of Snaefell and then continue

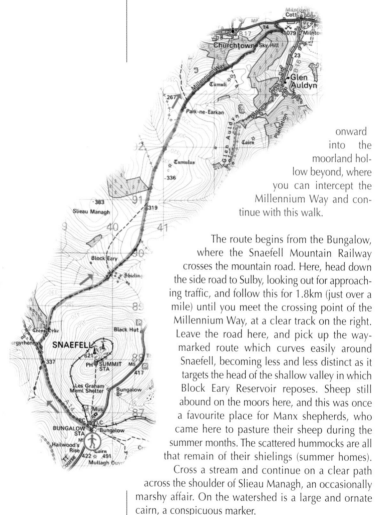

onward into the moorland hollow beyond, where you can intercept the Millennium Way and continue with this walk.

The route begins from the Bungalow, where the Snaefell Mountain Railway crosses the mountain road. Here, head down the side road to Sulby, looking out for approaching traffic, and follow this for 1.8km (just over a mile) until you meet the crossing point of the Millennium Way, at a clear track on the right. Leave the road here, and pick up the way-marked route which curves easily around Snaefell, becoming less and less distinct as it targets the head of the shallow valley in which Block Eary Reservoir reposes. Sheep still abound on the moors here, and this was once a favourite place for Manx shepherds, who came here to pasture their sheep during the summer months. The scattered hummocks are all that remain of their shielings (summer homes).

Cross a stream and continue on a clear path across the shoulder of Slieau Managh, an occasionally marshy affair. On the watershed is a large and ornate cairn, a conspicuous marker.

The route leads on to meet a track coming in from the right, from the Mountain Box on the TT course. Stay

The Millennium Way

Established in 1979, the Millennium Way was the first long distance footpath created on the island, and was timed to celebrate the Millennium Year of the Manx parliament, Tynwald. The path links Ramsey to Castletown, following as closely as possible the route of Manx kings through the centre of the island. (Ramsey was a safe anchorage, much favoured by the Norse kings; Castle Rushen in Castletown was the royal residence.) The route is an early highway with a long and ancient history. Once known as the Royal Way, it is recorded in the 13th-century Chronicles of the Kings of Mann and the Isles.

with the **Millennium Way** at this junction, which is now followed all the way to the end of the walk. From this point high on the moorland, the route is partially board-walked, and footpath restoration work was carried out here during 2002 and 2003.

The track continues to a metal gate in a wall. Beyond this it continues as a rough, stony track across heather moorland, and for a short stretch shares part of the Way with Walk 8. A wide sweep of moorland, patrolled by **hen harriers**, ravens and snipe, leads eventually to another metal gate and signpost ('Sky Hill 3m').

Hen harrier

While the hen harrier is now fairly widespread within the British Isles, its establishment on the Isle of Man is a great success story. Hen harriers began nesting here in 1977, usually in old conifer plantations. More than 40 pairs are breeding here currently, with more than 80 assembling to roost during the winter in what has become the largest hen harrier communal roost in western Europe at the Ballaugh Curraghs.

The descending path is a pleasure to follow, flanked high up on the moors by gorse and heather. Lower down it becomes gullied and then gradually twists down along the edge of Ballakillingan Plantation before reaching and passing a row of lovely beech trees as it crosses through Skyhill Wood. 'Sky Hill' is derived from 'Skogarfjall', meaning 'wooded hill'.

Sky Hill

In 1079, the Battle of Sky Hill took place on ground to the south of the Sulby–Ramsey road. The Chronicle of the Kings of Mann and the Isles record that a Norseman, Godred Crovan, mustered a great number of ships and came to Mann where he joined battle with King Fingal and the people of the land. Defeated twice, on the third attempt he landed his army by night at Ramsey, and hid 300 men in the woods of Sky Hill. Next day, at the height of the battle, the hidden forces attacked the Manxmen from behind and victory for Godred was assured. He treated the islanders mercifully, and established the Norse dynasty that ruled Mann until 1265. Godred is thought by some to be the 'King Orry' of Manx tradition, though others question whether the king existed at all. The Sky Hill battle is significant in Manx lore because, although the date of the first national Tynwald cannot be ascertained, it is thought that it might have been following Godred's conquest of the island. Set against this, the island celebrated 1000 years of unbroken parliamentary rule in 1979, which clearly suggests an earlier date than Godred's battle at Sky Hill. Indeed, the establishment of the Tynwald is credited to the time when the Kingdom of the Sudreys, which comprised the Outer Hebrides and the Isle of Man, came into being; thought to be in the 970s.

The view from **Sky Hill** is especially agreeable. Jurby church, white-painted, stands conspicuously on the coastline, while northwards across the sea lie the hills of Galloway, including Cairnsmore of Fleet and The Merrick. The Point of Ayre lighthouse just gets in on the act, clinging to the northern tip of the island and peeping over the low-lying Bride Hills. Further east the Lakeland fells of Cumbria present familiar hills viewed from an unfamiliar angle.

The track eventually curves down to meet the road. Cross with care, and turn right for about 500m to reach the turning into Glen Auldyn, where the walk ends. There are fairly regular bus services along the Sulby Glen road into Ramsey, which is little more than 1km (½ mile) further on.

WALK 15
Glen Wyllin

Distance:	6.5km (4 miles)
Map:	Isle of Man Outdoor Leisure Map: North
Start/Finish:	Glen Wyllin (grid ref 314902)
Parking:	Lower Glen Wyllin
Refreshments:	Kirk Michael

This easy walk follows farm access tracks and lanes, and takes the opportunity to cross over into the adjacent Glen Mooar in order to visit Spooyt Vane, one of the highest waterfalls on the island. A return is then made along the beach, using a section of the coastal path.

Leave the car park and head back to the Peel road. Cross and continue into the upper part of the glen where you find the Cooildarry Nature Reserve. Just before this the track bears right, heading uphill, and eventually levelling and becoming surfaced. When this meets a country lane – one that links Glen Mooar and Little London – turn right, walking downhill.

Go as far as a small **chapel** and then turn left to pass a car park, beyond which the lane deteriorates, becoming rough underfoot and often muddy. It leads to a footbridge, over which Glen Mooar is reached, close by the Spooyt Vane.

Patrick's Chapel

In the central part of Glen Mooar lie the remains of Cabbal Pherick (Patrick's Chapel), an early Christian chapel dating from the 8th–10th century. Now it is little more than a low-lying outline of the *keeill* (chapel) and surrounding burial ground and the remains of a priest's cell.

Walk down through Glen Mooar to reach the Peel road once more and cross into the descending lane opposite to reach the beach at the mouth of Glen Mooar. Now turn right along the beach, as far as Glen Wyllin, to complete the walk. Very occasionally (for instance during very high tides or really bad weather), it becomes difficult, if not impossible, to walk along the beach. If this is the case, simply retreat to the Peel road, turn left (towards Kirk Michael) and take the first turning on the right. This narrow lane, within 300m, reaches the old railway line, which can be joined and followed back to Glen Wyllin.

Note: The start of the old railway trackbed, which is the key to the alternative finish into Glen Wyllin, and the small chapel at which a turning was made towards Glen Mooar, are only 300m apart, enabling Glen Mooar to be omitted and a quicker return made to Glen Wyllin for those that need it.

WALK 16

Sulby Reservoir

Distance:	3km (1¾ miles) or 12km (7½ miles)
Map:	Isle of Man Outdoor Leisure Map: North
Start/Finish:	Sulby Reservoir car park (grid ref 374890)
Parking:	At start
Refreshments:	Pub in Sulby Glen

The short version of this walk is perfect for a warm summer's afternoon, before or after a picnic. It is nowhere demanding, and leads through a sizeable pine plantation onto the edge of open moorland, with lovely views. The longer version isn't significantly more demanding, just longer.

Druidale Farm, Sulby Glen

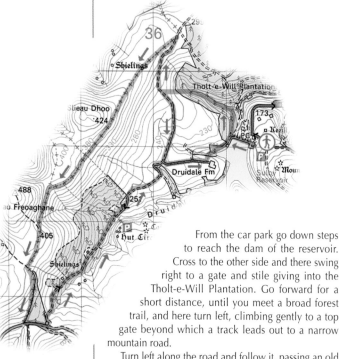

From the car park go down steps to reach the dam of the reservoir. Cross to the other side and there swing right to a gate and stile giving into the Tholt-e-Will Plantation. Go forward for a short distance, until you meet a broad forest trail, and here turn left, climbing gently to a top gate beyond which a track leads out to a narrow mountain road.

Turn left along the road and follow it, passing an old lime kiln, until you reach the turning down to Druidale Farm. Leave the road here by walking down the farm access track.

Just before you reach the farm, go left at a signpost, through a metal gate and down an enclosed path to another gate. Ahead lies a footbridge spanning an arm of the reservoir, with an awkward little mossy gully between it and the gate. Take care going down here and, once over the footbridge, bear right through another gate and along a pathway through bracken. This leads to a broad gate, just above the reservoir edge and giving into the Tholt-e-Will Plantation.

Through the gate, go only as far as the stile and gate at which you first entered the plantation. Turn right there, and recross the dam to complete the walk.

Alternative route: On reaching the mountain road, turn right and follow this for about 1km (⅔ mile), as far as a broad track on the left. Double back along this to a gate and then continue across the flank of Slieau Dhoo to meet a broad stony track just below Slieau Freoghane. Turn left again and follow this track southwards around Slieau Freoghane and the adjacent Sartfell to meet a road at the edge of Sartfell Plantation.

Turn left, ignore the branching road on the right, and continue to the far side of the plantation, where a road branches left – the other end of the same road you were on earlier. Go along this as far as the turning to Druidale Farm, and there turn right to complete the walk as described above.

On a clear day it is an easy matter to include both Slieau Freoghane and Sartfell in this walk, by easy and obvious diversions. That onto Slieau Freoghane is the steeper of the two.

WALK 17
Peel Hill and Corrins Hill

Distance:	5km (3 miles)
Map:	Isle of Man Outdoor Leisure Map: South
Start/Finish:	Peel Castle (grid ref 241843)
Parking:	Peel Castle

This short walk over the twin-topped hill that dominates the harbour town of Peel, and to a good extent protects it from southwesterlies, is quite exhilarating and, after an energetic beginning, soon takes to the seaward side of the hill before winding down to the inland valley road. The views are outstanding and embrace southern Scotland and the Mountains of Mourne in Northern Ireland.

Peel Castle

Peel

Considered by many to be the most 'Manx' of the island's towns, Peel and the historic St Patrick's Isle, is an ideal town to explore, full of narrow lanes with buildings of character and indeterminate history. All roads here lead to the harbour, emphasising the town's importance, then and now, as a centre for the Manx fishing industry. Visitors to Peel should seek out the award-winning House of Manannan, adjacent to the harbour, and a perfect place to learn about the history of the Isle of Man from the earliest settlers to the present day.

From the car park near Peel Castle head onto a broad, gravel track climbing onto Peel Hill and follow this to an obvious col between Peel Hill and the more southerly Corrins Hill. Here, at the col, the Raad ny Foillan (the coastal path) crosses in the form of a broad grassy path. Bear right onto this for a spectacular terraced walk high above the sea cliffs of Cashtal Mooar. This spins along in delightful fashion and, near Contrary Head, it divides. Keep left, gradually rounding the southern end of Corrins Hill and starting to head back towards **Peel**.

You leave the Raad ny Foillan at this point (which dashes off to the right). Instead, keep left, walking alongside a wall and, when this bears right, go with it, descending to a ladder-stile giving onto a short lane leading down to a farmhouse.

At the farmhouse turn left onto a broad track and then follow an obvious course winding down to meet a road. Turn left, almost immediately crossing a road bridge, but, on the other side, turn right down wooden steps to meet the River Neb near an old watermill.

Here, double back left to go under the road bridge, now following the course of an old railway trackbed that guides you

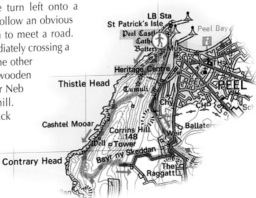

Peel Castle

The castle of Peel Island was built by William le Scrope, King of Mann from 1392 until 1399, who later became Earl of Wiltshire and treasurer to Richard II. Ostensibly, the castle was built to defend the cathedral here, which had been sacked by the Earl of Galloway in 1388. The castle is simple in design, consisting of a fortified gateway and a keep – quite a barrier if you imagine the modern causeway to be no longer there – with a red sandstone curtain wall.

For his support of Richard II, Scrope paid with his life at the hands of Henry IV, who gave the island to Henry Percy, Duke of Northumberland. But the Percys rebelled against Henry and after their defeat in 1403 the island was given to the first of the Stanleys, Sir John, for life, later confirmed in perpetuity, though Sir John never actually visited the island. But the move in effect brought the uneasy days of Manx history to a close. The Stanley family ruled as the Kings of Mann for 350 years.

back to the outskirts of Peel, past its power station, and finally reaching the end of the elongated harbour at another road bridge. Cross the bridge and follow the road towards **Peel Castle** and the start of the walk.

Alternative start: An alternative start may be made from the seafront at Peel, by following the road to the harbour and then left to the road bridge at the harbour's end. Cross the bridge and go immediately left onto a way-marked path steeply ascending to the col between Peel Hill and Corrins Hill, where the original route is joined.

The coastline below Corrins Hill

WALK 18

Glen Maye, the coast path and Patrick

Distance:	11km (6¾ miles)
Map:	Isle of Man Outdoor Leisure Map: South
Start/Finish:	Glen Maye (grid ref 236798)
Parking:	Opposite Waterfall Hotel
Refreshments:	Waterfall Hotel

This delightful walk begins by heading north along the coastal path before diving inland to visit to the small village of Kirk Patrick and its Church of the Holy Trinity. An ancient track then leads across upland pastures before returning along a quiet lane to Glen Maye.

From the Glen Maye car park go down steps into the top end of the glen and soon cross a bridge above the waterfall. Take the steps descending to the base of the waterfall and then continue on a riverside path. Lower down the glen, at a path junction, remain with the riverside path to reach the waterwheel. Here, leave the glen by turning up

The coast at Glen Maye

73

to a gate and then cross a road and go up the signposted path opposite (for Peel), which here is both the Raad ny Foillan and the Bayr ny Skeddan. The path climbs briefly and, not far above the bay, branches. Bear right, as the path then adopts a superb line across the top of cliffs and headlands, constantly undulating and changing direction in a way that makes the walk invigorating and encouraging. A pair of binoculars would be useful on this walk, as the cliffs are popular with a whole range of birds from the fairly commonplace herring gull, to kittiwake, fulmar, chough, stonechat and partridge, though the latter prefer the adjacent fields.

Simply keep going along the coastal path – you don't have a choice – until you meet a metal kissing-gate at the northern end of Corrins Hill, the prominent folly-topped hill that has been in view since near the start of the walk and which stands guardian over the town of Peel. Through the gate, bear right on a grassy track that soon merges with another and bears round to run alongside a wall, heading towards the folly. When the path and wall change direction, do likewise,

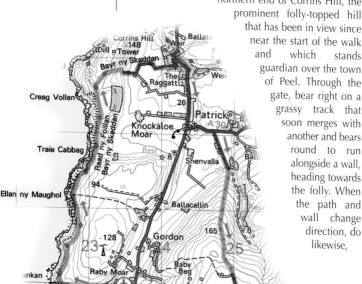

74

descending to a ladder-stile giving onto a rough, descending path leading down to a small row of houses.

At the houses, take the track going left and follow this through numerous twists and turns (all obvious) until, finally, it slips down to meet the Peel–Glen Maye road. Turn right and walk along the road as far as Kirk Patrick, and there take the side road signposted for St John's. The parish church is soon reached on the left, and has some interesting stained glass windows depicting scenes from the bible as well as Manx saints.

Continue past the church for about 300m and then leave the road by turning right onto a greenway road, setting off initially as a surfaced lane. When the surfacing ends, a rough track continues, climbing steadily throughout its length, flanked by drystone walls and gorse bushes, and offering a fine retrospective view of Peel and Corrins Hill.

Eventually the track emerges onto a surfaced lane. Here turn right and follow the lane, a generally quiet and peaceful prospect, all the way back to Glen Maye. On entering the village, near the post office, bear left down Hillside Terrace to return to the start.

Coastal cliffs above Glen Maye

WALK 19
Port Erin to Peel

Distance:	22km (13⅔ miles)
Map:	Isle of Man Outdoor Leisure Map: South
Start:	Port Erin (grid ref 196692)
Parking:	Near lifeboat station: Disc parking zones on streets
Refreshments:	Pubs and cafés in Port Erin
Finish:	Peel Castle (grid ref 241843)
Parking:	Peel Castle
Refreshments:	Various cafés and pubs in Peel

This is an outstanding walk, which, taken in full, demands a good deal of stamina as it involves three significant ascents, two from sea level. The coastal scenery throughout is of the highest order, the birdlife is diverse, the wild flowers likewise, and the walk a long succession of pleasures that make turning round and walking back the next day a tempting proposition. Failing that, you'll need to organise transport either to take you to the start or pick you up as a rather steamy roadside bundle near Peel Castle. Public transport, of course, serves both towns extremely well. The walk begins by tackling Bradda Head and the subsequent and higher Bradda Hill. From there a lovely descent sweeps down to Fleshwick Bay before

Note: Map continues on page 79

engaging low gear for the pull onto Lhiattee ny Beinnee. Another plunging descent brings you out to the road at the Sloc before romping to the high point of the walk, Cronk ny Arrey Laa. From here you next head down to sea level at Niarbyl from where an easy walk leads to the mouth of Glen Maye. But even there you haven't finished, for more coastal walking leads north to Corrins Hill beyond which lies Peel Castle and the end of the day.

Leave Port Erin by walking up the main road towards the conspicuous tower on Bradda Head. Quit the road at the arched entrance to Bradda Glen and follow a delightful path through the glen until a sign directs you up to the Coronation Footpath, reached up steps and through a wall gap. Turn left onto a broad green track that leads to a wooden kissing-gate, beyond which it climbs steadily beside a wall towards Milner Tower. When the wallside path meets a fence, go forward through a metal kissing-gate and turn right up a stony track, which leads up to the tower.

Looking back to Bradda Hill from Niarbyl

From the tower, a clear track descends to a nearby metal gate and signpost, but, for those not of a nervous disposition, a narrow track hugs the top edge of the sea cliffs and provides some spectacular views, not only of the cliffs, but of the numerous sea birds that frequent them. Close by, a plaque announces that a short distance away the winner of the Kodak 'World's Best Photograph' competition was taken! Today, you might gaze out over sea cliffs and wonder what was so special. But the photographer, C. W. Powell of Manchester, took a photograph of his fiancée in the sunset and won prize money of £20,000.

Eventually the path leads to less intimidating ground, but continues to parallel the sea cliffs, now climbing steadily as it mounts the heather shoulder of Bradda Hill. At first the path courts an old fenceline (on the left) but, at a wall corner and stile, switches sides and then follows a wall almost to the summit of the hill.

A brief diversion is needed to reach the summit cairn on Bradda Hill, one of only five Marilyns on the island, such being a hill that is at least 500ft (roughly 150m) higher than the land around it.

From the top of Bradda Hill take the obvious path heading down towards unseen Fleshwick Bay. It drops quite steeply to a wall gap, with good views northwards to Niarbyl Bay, and then continues, still descending through heather, to reach the bottom edge of Fleshwick Plantation.

Go forward along a field edge to reach a narrow lane leading to the left down to Fleshwick Bay, but just before reaching the bay, step right over a small stream and begin quite a steep climb, initially alongside a fence, but then linking footpath signposts along a clear path that swings about to take the sting out of the ascent. If in doubt, keep going up, and this dubious technique – though adequate here – will eventually intercept a broad and clear track across the top of the mountain, Lhiattee ny Beinnee, an elongated ridge topped by a cairn of large quartz boulders.

Continue in the same direction and gradually come onto a descending stretch, with lovely coastal views. The path drops steadily through heather and reaches another road at a conspicuous bend; this is the Sloc. Go through the road gate and then immediately left through another beside it. Then turn right, passing a small hillock to begin the long pull up onto Cronk ny Arrey Laa. The way is marked by poles, though none is needed as the route is very direct and very clear, leading unerringly to a huge cairn on the summit of the hill.

Although there is little to see on the ground, the small hillock passed at the start of this section is the site of

Note: Map continues on page 80

Cronk ny Arrey Laa
The summit of Cronk ny Arrey Laa is a prehistoric burial mound dating from the early Bronze Age. It was excavated in 1958. The summit is known as a Watch Hill, part of a defensive line of hills along the western coast of the island. From the top of the hill there is a spectacular view of most of the southern part of the island, so being a watchman was a responsible position with harsh penalties for failure to be on duty or for sleeping while on duty: these ranged from forfeiting 'bodye and goodes', to a 'cowe' and 'lyfe and lyme'.

a Pictish village, also once occupied by neolithic farmers who built a defensive stronghold on the hill, surrounded by a wooden palisade and a ditch. The outline of the dwellings can be seen from the slopes of **Cronk ny Arrey Laa**.

This far the walk has followed the coastal path, the Raad ny Foillan, the Way of the Gulls, but for a while now we leave it by turning east from the top of Cronk ny Arrey Laa, passing the trig pillar and heading down a clear and broad track to reach the road again. Turn left and, about 100m later, branch left (in effect keep forward) onto a broad, walled track. This leads down around Eary Cushlin to reach a track junction at the edge of Kerroodhoo Plantation. Keep forward, initially alongside the plantation, then moving slightly away from it, but eventually descending a stony gully to reach houses at a road end. Here, turn left to follow a waymarked route around field edges that eventually descends to arguably the most beautiful spot on the whole island, Niarbyl Bay.

Delightful every step of the way, the path teases a route around sea cliffs and drops to a stony bay, used as a film location for the 'Irish-set' film *Waking Ned*. Continue with the obvious path and soon reach the charming niche at Niarbyl where 'Ned Devine's' thatched cottage sits beside an ancient cannon.

A bit of road walking now ensues. Turn up the road serving Niarbyl and walk up to Dalby – a conveniently placed pub – the Ballacallin – would be a good place to break for lunch.

Turn left along the road and follow this for about 1.6km (1 mile), now once more on the Raad ny Foillan. At Cronkmoar the path leaves the road at the side of a house and pursues a signposted route down to the mouth of Glen Maye – the yellow glen. Why yellow? Visit in summer and see for yourself: gorse, everywhere, and beautiful it is, too.

On reaching Glen Maye it is possible to cross the in-flowing stream and make a steep and direct assault on the headland on the other side. But it is much easier to turn right and walk up the glen for a short distance, sticking with the signposted coastal path, which is now also

Cottage at Niarbyl (used in Waking Ned*)*

part of the Bayr ny Skeddan, and shortly turning left onto a gently rising path.

The path climbs briefly and, not far above the bay, branches. Bear right as the path then adopts a superb line across the top of cliffs and headlands, constantly undulating and changing direction in a way that makes the walk invigorating and encouraging. This is where a pair of binoculars come into their own. A wide range of birds can be seen on the cliffs, from herring gulls to kittiwakes and fulmars. Choughs and stonechats are also a common sight and partridges are no strangers to the adjacent fields.

Simply keep going along the coastal path – you don't have a choice – until you meet a metal kissing-gate at the northern end of Corrins Hill, the prominent folly-topped hill that has been in view since near the start of the walk and which stands guardian over the town of Peel. Through the gate, bear right on a grassy track that soon merges with another and bears round to run alongside a wall, heading towards the folly. As the wall turns abruptly to the right, leave it by going forward onto Corrins Hill.

Cross the hill and begin an easy descent towards Peel Castle. A number of routes now come and go, but it is not difficult to figure out the easiest way down, a route that emerges at a car park at Fenella Beach, one of the smallest on the island. Peel Castle stands near by, and marks the end of the walk, but is well worth a visit, providing, as it does, a relaxing end to the day.

WALK 20
Cregneash and Mull Hill

Distance:	2km (1 mile)
Map:	Isle of Man Outdoor Leisure Map: South
Start/Finish:	Cregneash (grid ref 191674)
Parking:	At start
Refreshments:	Café in Cregneash

This brief walk is an introduction to one of the most fascinating parts of the Isle of Man, the Meayll Peninsula, where the village of Cregneash re-creates life as it was in Man and the prehistoric remains on Mull (Meayll) Hill tell of even earlier times. The view from the top of Mull Hill is extensive, embracing the whole of the southern part of the island and the Calf of Man. Further away, the mountains of North Wales can be seen, as well as those of Northern Ireland and southern Scotland.

Cregneash village

83

Begin from the **Cregneash** village car park in the old quarry and turn right towards the village. Just at the village road sign bear left onto a descending track that leads to the centre of the village. The village today is a living museum, and while you can wander freely along the roads, it is only on payment at the entrance that you can enter the buildings and learn about life here.

Leave the village by returning to the main road (go up past the green telephone box) and turn left along the road until you can branch to the right onto a single track road flanked by gorse bushes. Follow this lane as far as a wide, grassy lay-by on the right-hand side. Up above, you can see a fenced area. Take the footpath up to this and, over a step-stile, enter the grounds of the **Meayll stone circle**.

After exploring the area go across another stile at the back, and walk onto the top of Mull Hill, site of a Second World War radar station. Continue through this to locate a prominent and broad gravel track that curves back down to the single track road. Turn left onto it and left again to return to the village. Remain on the main road to reach the parking area.

Cregneash

The tiny village of Cregneash is isolated from the rest of Man, and was the last stronghold of the traditional skills and customs that characterised the crofting way of life. A small community of hardy people prospered here from the middle of the 17th century, combining small-scale farming and other diverse occupations. During the fishing seasons, men here would leave the fields for the trials of the Scottish and Irish waters.

At Cregneash today, the evidence of this rugged lifestyle is re-created by Manx National Heritage, and features Harry Kelly's cottage, opened in 1938, and portraying today the way of life on the island 150 years ago. Parts of the village featured in the film *Waking Ned*. It is not so long since all the buildings here were thatched, but now only a few remain so.

St Peter's Church

For many years, the people of Cregneash did not have a church in the village. This perturbed the vicar of Rushen because the people of Cregneash had to walk to his church in all weathers. So, he began holding a service one night a week in one of the village houses. By the mid-1870s, the new vicar encouraged the people of Cregneash to build a church of their own, which they did: everyone gave their labour free, with the result that the church's only expense was for materials (about £150). The church was dedicated to St Peter by the Bishop of Sodor and Man on 13th December 1878, but only the sanctuary was consecrated so that the rest of the building could be used as a school.

The Meayll Circle

Meayll Circle

The 'Circle of Stones' is a series of tombs now dated to 3500 BC, the middle neolithic age. It was excavated originally in 1893, when cremated human bones, pottery, jet and flints were found. Further excavations produced numerous urns with ashes and charcoal, knives and pebbles.

The circle is elliptical and consists of six structures (called tritaphs), which were used as burial chambers. Modern research suggests that cremation would have taken place away from the site and the ashes placed in urns before being carried ceremonially for interment here.

WALK 21

Glen Maye, Niarbyl Bay and Dalby Mountain

Distance:	11km (6¾ miles)
Map:	Isle of Man Outdoor Leisure Map: South
Start/Finish:	Glen Maye (grid ref 236798)
Parking:	Opposite Waterfall Hotel
Refreshments:	Waterfall Hotel

Glen Maye is one of the most beautiful of the Manx National Glens and Niarbyl Bay among the most tranquil and relaxing places on the island. Combining both with a return across the internationally rare habitat of mountain heath that comprises Dalby Mountain brings together three very potent elements that hallmark all that is outstanding about walking on this modestly sized island.

From the car park go down steps into the top end of the glen and soon cross a bridge above the waterfall. Take the steps descending to the base of the waterfall and then, having viewed it, continue on a riverside path. Lower down the glen, at a path junction, remain with the riverside path to reach the waterwheel. Here, leave the glen by turning up to a gate and then head left onto a narrow track starting down the narrowing glen, flanked, especially on the right, by high cliffs on which breeding fulmars can often be seen in the early summer.

Niarbyl

On reaching the bay, where the Rushen meets the sea, turn sharply up to the left onto a path ascending the headland. This leads to a gate giving into a large pasture, go forward up the right-hand edge to a signpost sending the path to the right along a sunken path flanked by gorse and wind-blown hawthorn. At the end of the path turn left, up another. At the top turn right through a metal kissing-gate and go forward alongside a gorse hedgerow, eventually to arrive at another kissing-gate giving onto an enclosed path leading out to the Dalby–Glen Maye road. (Anyone wanting a really short walk should turn

87

left here and follow the road back to **Glen Maye**.) Turn right and follow the road to the village of Dalby, turning right opposite the Ballacallin Hotel onto a descending road to Niarbyl.

On reaching Niarbyl, with its attractive thatched cottage, branch left onto a rising path onto the headland above the bay. With numerous retrospective views of Niarbyl Bay, the path flirts with clifftop edges, wanders down steps to another cove and along its shore, then starts climbing again, this time on a broader track. Go past a bench (ideally placed for a breather) and keep forward up a flight of steps.

Immediately after a fence gap, leave the main path going forward and bear left onto a waymarked path, narrow and climbing. At the top of the climb, turn left over a stile beside a waymark and go forward alongside a post and wire fence to a kissing-gate. Through this go forward along a grassy path at the top edge of a field, which leads out to a gate and ladder-stile. Over this, turn right onto an ascending rocky path. Climb to a ladder-stile at a signpost where the Raad ny Foillan branches right below Creagan Mooar Brooghs, and here leave the coastal path by bearing left up a stony path ascending through gorse.

Climb to go past a gate, continuing with the track, which is now running parallel with the edge of Kerroodhoo Plantation on the left. At the next gate the track finally reaches the plantation edge, which it accompanies to meet a surfaced lane at the top edge of the plantation. Turn left onto the lane and follow it out to meet a road.

Glen Maye National Glen

Glen Maye, or Glen Mea, the luxuriant glen, as it was once known, comprises almost 5ha (12 acres), situated on either side of the Rushen River and contains a splendid waterfall. In the lower paddock is the Mona Erin Wheelcase, the only extant evidence of mining that took place here between 1740 and 1870. Although lead was found, it was generally poor quality and in insufficient quantities to support a major industry. Most of the trees in the glen are sycamore, elm or ash, with some reintroduced oak.

Dalby Mountain Nature Reserve

This 28.4ha (70-acre) reserve comprises traditional heather moorland and is popular with a wide range of bird species including red grouse, hen harrier, curlew, snipe, skylark, meadow pipit and wheatear. Patches of the wet heath are dominated by ling, purple moor grass and rushes, and bog asphodel. Other species include devil's bit scabious, cross-leaved heath and several orchids. The reserve has over 5 per cent of the island's wet heath and is an internationally rare habitat.

At the road junction head left for about 200m and there leave the road by turning right onto a signposted track heading out on the **Dalby Mountain Nature Reserve**. The rutted track is flanked by heather, which in autumn is a delight to see. In the distance, the tower on Corrins Hill above Peel eases into view.

Eventually the moorland track descends to a track junction. Here, go forward through a gate and onto a continuing sunken track. The course of the track across the moors is always clear and, beyond the gate, undergoes a number of transformations from wide grassy swards to narrow rocky gullies flowing with water, but always heading in a clear direction. This is a delightfully robust section of the walk and ends at a metal gate giving onto a lane at the edge of Glen Maye village. Turn left and follow the lane out to the main valley road. Bear right and follow the road for what is the short distance back to the starting point at the head of Glen Maye.

WALK 22
Corlea and South Barrule

Distance:	8.2km (5 miles)
Map:	Isle of Man Outdoor Leisure Map: South
Start/Finish:	South Barrule Plantation (grid ref 275767)
Parking:	At start

I may be alone in this, but I experience a peculiar sense of privilege when I find myself in the middle of some prehistoric settlement, like the Iron Age hill fort encountered on the highest point of this walk. It's the notion that prehistoric man may well have perched on the same rock as me eating the Iron Age equivalent of a pork pie and pickled egg and almost certainly gazing out across a landscape that, apart from the missing trees and the masts on Snaefell, would not have been noticeably different from the view you see today. There is a fair amount of free range wandering on this walk, through acres of heather, but none of it is especially difficult, except after prolonged rain. But if all you want is to tick off another Marilyn then refer to Walk 40; this walk is for those who like to wander 'lonely as a cloud'.

South Barrule

The walk begins from the car park at the entrance to
the South Barrule Plantation on the Foxdale side
of the hill. Go to the back of the car park,
through a gate and take the left-hand one
of two broad tracks continuing into the
plantation. This track roughly
parallels the
Castletown
road and, in
due course,
emerges from
the trees onto
a narrow sur-
faced lane. Turn
left for a few
strides and then,
just before reaching
the road, turn right onto a
continuing plantation track.

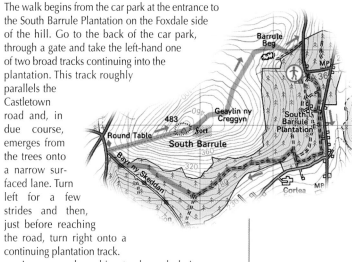

Ignore any branching tracks and obvious access
points, but continue always within the plantation
boundary, even when it changes direction. (Note: There
is some confusion between the plantation tracks shown
on the map and how they actually appear on the
ground, but this doesn't significantly affect things, it just
makes you wonder!)

In due course, the track comes to an obvious track
junction. Left is a way out of the plantation to a road
(grid ref 272755); right, the track climbs gently into the
plantation. Turn right, uphill, but only for about 200m,
and then go left on another plantation track that
quite soon emerges into a more recently planted area,
with (for the time being) fine views south to Derby
Haven and Langness.

A short way on you reach a gate at the entrance to
the Corlea Plantation, from where the ongoing track is a
delight to follow. Because the plantation is more open,
so you see a wider range of birdlife, with stonechat,
wheatear, warblers and the occasional visiting hen harrier putting in an appearance.

91

South Barrule hill fort

A fine Celtic Iron Age hill fort encloses the summit of South Barrule, at 483m (1585ft) the main defensive stronghold in the south of the island in prehistoric times, and the highest and largest hill fort on the island. The original inner rampart was largely destroyed, but encloses the remains of many circular huts. The fort was later enlarged by the construction of massive outer stone ramparts, and partially excavated 1960–61 and 1968. It bears many similarities with pre-Roman tribal hill forts found in southern Britain.

When the track forks at a distinct junction, branch right. A little distance further on, at another meeting of tracks, keep forward onto a track/path that leads through a wide firebreak, more or less contouring across the southern slopes of South Barrule.

The path through the firebreak eventually climbs gently to run along the top boundary of the plantation, and leads to a stile in a fence corner, beyond which lies a rough track used by the Bayr ny Skeddan. Turn right onto this and, just before reaching a road, leave the track at a kissing gate for a clear path striking up the south-west ridge of South Barrule. The angle is not so daunting as it seems end on, and a brisk walk will bring you to the summit in less than half an hour.

From the summit continue in the same direction as on the ascent. A path begins the descent through heather. You pass down through the **hill fort** outer defences, and continue to a large boulder where the now-narrow path divides. Here branch left, but soon the path runs blind, leaving you to figure out the easiest way on. The blanket heather is short and there are numerous sheep tracks as well as the occasional vehicle track to ease progress. Initially, a useful target is the masted summit of Snaefell in the far distance, or the Kionslieu Reservoir, rather nearer and visible to the right of Barrule Beg, the subsidiary top of South Barrule.

Soon you see the top of the South Barrule Plantation with a quarry to its left. This too is a useful target, but you need to keep to the left of the quarry, so a rough bearing on Barrule Beg is the best way down.

Eventually you meet a fence (before crossing onto Barrule Beg), and if you follow this to the right you will come to a fence corner just above the quarry. Here an old gate enables you to continue downhill alongside the top edge of the quarry (fence). When the fence changes direction, keep on for a little while longer, but gradually work down through deeper heather to a cluster of sheep pens close by the quarry access track.

At the sheep pens you can find a way to a wooden gate giving onto a vehicle track, which takes you down to the quarry access and then out to the road. Turn right, walking downhill to return to the car park at the start of the walk.

On the slopes of South Barrule

WALK 23

Glen Maye to Glen Rushen by Dalby Mountain

Distance:	10km (6¼ miles)
Map:	Isle of Man Outdoor Leisure Map: South
Start/Finish:	Glen Maye (grid ref 236798)
Parking:	Opposite Waterfall Hotel
Refreshments:	Waterfall Hotel

This fine circuit of Dalby Mountain Nature Reserve begins in the village of Glen Maye. When you learn that 'maye' is Manx for 'yellow', and see the vast swathes of gorse that cloak the hillsides here, you'll understand where the name came from. But this walk heads away from Glen Maye onto the neighbouring expanse of Dalby Mountain – a significant nature reserve of prime heathland – before turning back towards Glen Maye to pass the old slate quarries of Glen Rushen.

Set off from the car park at Glen Maye and turn right, going down the road in the direction of Dalby until, after about 250m, you can branch left onto a narrow lane running alongside a stream. Follow this until, as you reach the last property, you can turn right (at a sign 'Unsuitable for Motor Vehicles') onto a sunken track.

The track climbs steadily and is initially narrow and flanked by embankments and hedgerows. Later it narrows even more before reaching level ground above. Farmland predominates for a while before the track finally reaches the edge of the Dalby Mountain Nature Reserve at a gate.

Here, go forward along a broad track cutting a line across the heather moorland, eventually to reach a road. Turn left and follow the road alongside the Glen Rushen Plantation until finally it reaches the crossroads, near the dome of South Barrule, known as the Round Table.

Route A: About 450m after joining the road from the heathland, it is possible to turn left onto the Bayr ny Skeddan on a signposted route that descends through the Lhargan Plantation and meets up with the main line on the edge of Glen Rushen. Taking this option would save you about 1.6km (1 mile).

Main walk contd: Continue up the road to Round Table, and turn left at the cross-roads. A few strides later branch left through a gate onto a greenway road descending towards the Round Table Plantation ahead. Another gate gives into this planta-tion, through which a clear, rutted path descends to another gate on the far side.

Now go for-ward into a path enclosed by low walls, passing a derelict croft and steadily following a clear track pass-ing below chim-neys and ruined buildings of an industrial past at Beckwith's Vein, one of the principal **lead mines** on the island. Soon you enter Glen Rushen shortly after linking up once more with the Bayr ny Skeddan.

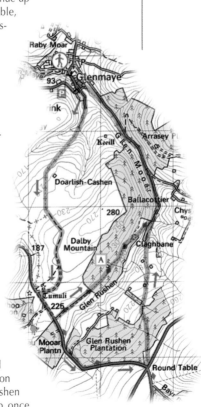

Now the old valley road, no longer used and becoming overgrown, takes the route through Glen Rushen for a little over 800m until a waymarked path descends on the left to run above the River Maye.

The path gradually descends to reach the riverbank and then crosses it by a footbridge. Over the bridge bear right through gorse. At a signpost turn left onto a broad track leading out to the lane used at the start of the walk. There turn right and walk out to join the Glen Maye to Dalby road, once more bearing right to walk back up to the Waterfall Hotel.

Lead mining

It is not known when lead mining started in the Isle of Man, though it is certainly the first recorded industry, a mining charter having been granted to the monks of Furness Abbey in 1246 by King Harald Olaffson. The Manx mining industry reached its zenith around the middle of the 19th century, with the main areas being at Laxey and Foxdale. The Foxdale vein runs almost east to west, with the most westerly vein being Beckwith's, above Glen Rushen, and encountered on this walk. The mine was sunk in 1881 following the chance discovery of a lump of galena (lead ore) by a man driving a hay cart. The shaft at Beckwith's descends 335m (1099ft). When you take into account that the mine buildings are only 180m (591ft) above sea level, it follows that the mine shaft descends to 155m (509ft) below sea level.

WALK 24
Cronk ny Arrey Laa

Distance:	4.5km (2¾ miles)
Map:	Isle of Man Outdoor Leisure Map: South
Start/Finish:	Road bend at grid ref 217733
Parking:	At start

This brief, but, be warned, steep ascent is deceptively simple. The summit played an important part in the history of the defence of the island, and its conquest today is well worth the effort.

Starting from the roadside parking area, cross to the right-hand one of two gates and, through this, turn right onto a rising grassy track passing to the right of a small hillock. You are following the Raad ny Foillan here and the route to the summit cairn is very clear and marked by poles for good measure.

From the top of the hill the simplest descent is back the way you came, but you can also branch off in an easterly direction on a very clear and direct path to meet a road. Once on the road, turn right and follow it back to the start. The road does have the advantage of some outstanding viewpoints embracing Port St Mary, Port Erin, the Calf of Man and the long ridge of Lhiattee ny Beinnee, but the disadvantage of passing traffic some of which regards this stretch of road as a race track.

Hut circles

From the slopes of Cronk ny Arrey Laa you can identify the outlines of a group of hut circles. There isn't much to see when you actually get there – you pass the small hillock at the start of the walk – but these are the remnants of a Pictish settlement. There was also a neolithic defensive site here, surrounded by wooden palisades and a ditch.

Cronk ny Arrey Laa from Lhiattee ny Beinnee

WALK 25

Lhiattee ny Beinnee and Fleshwick Bay

Distance:	8km (5 miles)
Map:	Isle of Man Outdoor Leisure Map: South
Start/Finish:	Road bend at grid ref 217733
Parking:	At start

This is a stunning walk every step of the way. The initial climb to the top of Lhiattee ny Beinnee is nothing like so daunting as it appears from the roadside and, once on top of the ridge, the walking is delightfully easy. The views, initially northwards towards Niarbyl Bay, are impressive and improve once the route descends to bring Fleshwick Bay in on the act. By a round-about route, the walk returns across the heather moorland of Lhiattee ny Beinnee's eastern flanks.

Begin from the parking space at the road-side and cross to the left-hand one of two gates opposite, which gives access to one of the island's green-way roads, Bayr Glass, along which this walk will conclude. Through the gate go forward on a narrow path through heather leading to the steep northern slopes Lhiattee ny Beinnee. Follow a clear path, climbing steadily and with ever-improving views northwards to Niarbyl

Lhiattee ny Beinnee from the approach to Fleshwick Bay

Bay, ultimately to reach the large cairn of quartz boulders that marks the summit of this elongated mountain ridge. In late summer the ridge is a particular delight, a canvas of heather purple and gorse yellow highlighted by random tufts of cotton grass.

The ongoing track traverses the summit ridge and then starts to descend as Port Erin, Port St Mary and the steep-sided defile of Fleshwick Bay come into view. Dropping more steeply, the path becomes directed by signposts down eventually to a wall corner and ladder-stile. Over the stile, continue descending to a signpost and then going down alongside a low wall at the head of Fleshwick Bay.

The path eventually reaches the edge of Fleshwick Bay where it meets a lane. The bay itself is sheltered and a popular place with divers, the waters are clear and the setting ideal for lazing away the day.

Turn left, following the lane for a few hundred metres, as far as a signposted path on the right. Leave the lane here and walk up to the lower edge of Fleshwick Plantation. Turn left along the foot of the plantation on a broad green track between drystone walls. Shortly, the path merges with a farm access track. Continue in the same direction, walking out through a gorse-studded landscape. Keep going as far as the first building on the left, just beyond which a signposted path branches sharply left.

Turn here and soon enter a rising pathway flanked by gorse that climbs to a surfaced lane. Keep ahead along this to meet a road and again go forward, continuing to a T-junction. Turn left (signposted 'Surby only') onto an ascending lane.

At the top of the lane, maintain the same direction, now on a bridleway leading to a gate giving onto the Bayr Glass, one of the Manx greenway roads. Through the gate strike out across open heathland, climbing steadily but not excessively. The track follows a delightful course across the eastern slopes of Lhiattee ny Beinnee, with superb forward views of Cronk ny Arrey Laa, and across the island to the distant settlement of Castletown.

Continue following the moorland track until it returns you to the starting point.

Fleshwick Bay

WALK 26
Bradda Hill

Distance:	5km (3 miles)
Map:	Isle of Man Outdoor Leisure Map: South
Start/Finish:	Port Erin (grid ref 196692)
Parking:	Near lifeboat station: Disc parking zones on streets
Refreshments:	Pubs and cafés in Port Erin

The 221m (725ft) of ascent, from sea level to the top of Bradda Hill can seem much more than it is on a hot day. But as a rule there's a sea breeze blowing and this helps enormously. The view from Bradda Head is outstanding and extends to the mountains of Northern Ireland as well as the coast of southern Scotland. For those who collect such summits, Bradda Hill is one of the island's Marilyns.

Leave Port Erin by walking up the main road towards the tower on Bradda Head. Turn off the road at the arched entrance to Bradda Glen, and follow a path through the glen until a sign directs you up to the Coronation

Bradda Glen

Milner Tower

The monument on the top of Bradda Head is dedicated to William Milner in grateful acknowledgement of his many charities to the poor of Port Erin, and for his never tiring efforts for the benefit of the Manx fishermen. Milner was a safe maker by profession, from Liverpool. He was instrumental in securing the erection of the breakwater at Port Erin. The tower was erected by public subscription in 1871, and when the foundation stone was laid, Milner threw a huge party to which, it seems, the whole neighbourhood was invited. The tower was completed during his lifetime and is said to be fashioned after one of his keys.

Footpath, reached up steps and through a wall gap. Turn left onto a broad green track that leads to a wooden kissing-gate beyond which it climbs steadily beside a wall towards **Milner Tower**.

When the wallside path meets a fence, go forward through a metal kissing-gate and turn right up a stony track that leads up to the tower.

From the tower a clear track descends to a nearby metal gate and signpost, but, for those not of a nervous disposition, a narrow track hugs the top edge of the sea cliffs and provides some spectacular views not only of the cliffs but of the numerous sea birds that frequent them.

Eventually the path leads to less intimidating ground, but continues to parallel the sea cliffs, now climbing steadily as it mounts the heather shoulder of Bradda Hill. At first the path courts an old fenceline (on the left) but, at a wall corner and stile, switches sides and then follows a wall almost to the summit of the hill.

*Milner Tower,
Bradda Hill*

A brief diversion is needed to reach the summit cairn on Bradda Hill, one of only five Marilyns on the island, such being a hill that is at least 500ft (roughly 150m) higher than the land around it.

From the top of Bradda Hill take the obvious path heading down towards unseen Fleshwick Bay. It drops quite steeply to a wall gap with good views northwards to Niarbyl Bay, and then continues, still descending through heather, to reach the bottom edge of Fleshwick Plantation. There turn right along a broad green track enclosed by walls.

Soon the track merges with a farm access track, which later runs on to meet the end of a surfaced lane (Ernie Broadbent Walk), and trots out to meet a road. Turn right into Bradda East, walking for about 200m, to a signposted path on the left, passing along a building gable onto an enclosed path along the edge of an arable field. Cross a stone step-stile and walk down the right-hand edge of a field.

Lower down the field another stile gives onto the edge of a golf course. Walk forward for a short distance, and then, when you reach a the corner of a wall, turn right, following the edge of the golf course (taking care to evade miss-hit golf balls – or, better, make sure that those who might hit them know you are there!) until, on the far side of the course, you can dip to the right along a narrow footpath to emerge at a road near a telephone box.

Turn left and follow the road back into Port Erin.

WALK 27

Port St Mary and Port Erin

Distance:	10.5km (6½ miles) plus 1.6km (1 mile) in Port St Mary
Map:	Isle of Man Outdoor Leisure Map: South
Start/Finish:	Port St Mary (grid ref 211671)
Parking:	Car park area along coast
Refreshments:	Port St Mary, The Sound (café), Port Erin
Note:	Between The Sound and Port Erin dogs are prohibited, even on leads.

This is one of the most pleasing walks in the book, taking in a section of the Raad ny Foillan (the coastal path) that is constantly changing direction and presenting new views, new panoramas and fresh cliffscapes. To complete the walk you'll need either to walk back from Port Erin to Port St Mary or, better (and the assumed option) take the short ride on the steam railway to Port St Mary Station and turn right on leaving the station for the 1.6km (1 mile) walk back to the starting point.

From the parking area turn left, walking away from Port St Mary until, after the last houses, you can go forward onto a broad track feeding into the edge of the golf course. Almost immediately branch left onto a path alongside a concrete wall, leading up to an estate road. Turn left, up the road, and shortly head into an estate through which the route is waymarked, and leads to an enclosed path cutting through to another road. Once more, turn left and keep following the road, which skims along above Perwick Bay, and is later signposted to **The Chasms**.

On reaching a track junction, maintain the same direction, going over a high ladder-stile beside a metal gate and continuing ahead on a rough track across a pasture to another ladder-stile. Stick with the ongoing track, which slices through a

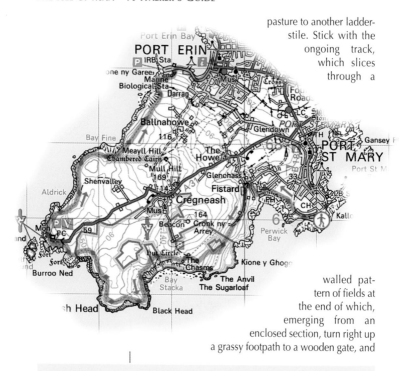

walled pattern of fields at the end of which, emerging from an enclosed section, turn right up a grassy footpath to a wooden gate, and

The Chasms

Formed by earth movement, the Chasms are a spectacular sight, terminating in the sea far below. Tradition holds that the cracks appeared when Jesus was crucified and the earth quaked. The whole headland is a mass of stunning cliffs in confusion and disarray; indeed the point Kione-y-ghoghan means 'headland of disorder'. Inevitably, the Chasms have attracted many stories. Here, for example, the Irish warriors who had assassinated King Olaf I in 1153 were captured by the Manx people and beheaded, their bodies flung into one of the chasms and soil tipped down on top of them, hence the name Skort Sidroryn, the chasm of the soldiers. Further on, another chasm is known as Skort Tashtey, the chasm of the treasure, an allusion to the belief than when the Countess of Derby was forced to quit the island in 1651, her treasure was hidden in the chasm. The story adds that the treasure has never been found.

then bear left towards a signpost and stile in a fence on the skyline to the left.

Do not cross the stile (which simply gives access to a viewing point for The Chasms), but instead turn right, walking uphill alongside a wall and then walk up towards what looks like a derelict house but which was the old Chasms café and is today a shelter.

Keep to the left, parallel with a wall, to reach a large stile giving onto the great expanse of Spanish Head, across which a clear footpath cuts through the heather and dwarf gorse. Ignore all branching footpaths and stick to the coastal path which clings to the top edge of the cliffs but later moves inland a little as it cuts across to the cliffs of Spanish Head, the southernmost tip of the Manx mainland.

An easy wander across the headlands soon brings the Calf of Man into view, with a clear path continuing through heather and gorse.

The path eventually drops to cross a small footbridge spanning a burn. Go over a step-stile and bear left to another, beyond which a path climbs onto a low headland before bending around a small cove, Carrick Nay. The ongoing path soon reaches a memorial and wanders across to the new café built at The Sound in 2002.

The Calf of Man from The Sound

Thousla Cross
The Thousla Cross, named after the tidal Thousla Rock just offshore, commemorates an act of heroism by men of Rushen parish in their rescue of the crew of the French schooner *Jeane St Charles*, in 1858. The ship was en route to Londonderry in Northern Ireland from Pontrieux, part of a trade that had flourished following the Crimean War, when it got into difficulties and was forced to drop anchor in the channel that separates the Isle of Man from the Calf of Man.

The Sound is a good place to take a break and it is not unusual to sit among the rocks here and watch a dozen or more grey seals bobbing in the choppy waters of the Little Sound keeping an eye on passers by.

Just beyond the café stands the **Thousla Cross**, from which you can walk up to a ladder stile. Beyond, the path steadily climbs around a headland, becoming narrower and more rocky as it passes Clett Aldrick. It climbs to a stile from which the ongoing path undulates alongside a clifftop fence through rock outcrops, heather and gorse. Keep an eye open in springtime and early summer for the delicate squill, which grows profusely around here. The walking is easy and delightful, everything that clifftop walking should be.

Gradually, as Port Erin comes into view, the path starts to descend, eventually going down to a wooden kissing-gate at the end of a fence. Continue descending alongside a fence until it changes direction and becomes enclosed between a fence and drystone wall. This in turn leads to a metal gate beyond which the path descends towards the lifeboat station, there to meet a road. Turn right and walk into Port Erin.

The railway station is in the main street, at right angles to the beach. Trains operate between the middle of April and late October, and the current timetable is available from all tourist information offices. The journey takes about 5 minutes.

On arrival at Port St Mary Station simply turn right out of the station and follow the main road into town, maintaining roughly the same direction throughout finally to emerge at the southern edge of the bay.

WALK 28

Colby Glen, Ballakilpheric and Bay ny Carrickey

Distance:	6.5km (4 miles)
Map:	Isle of Man Outdoor Leisure Map: South
Start/Finish:	Bay ny Carrickey (grid ref 234687)
Parking:	Roadside parking area
Refreshments:	Pubs at Colby and 1km (½ mile) west of start

The attractive Colby Glen is just north of the village and centres on Colby River, a delightful burn flowing through a narrow, wooded gorge, which in springtime boasts lovely displays of bluebells and primroses. This walk passes Colby Station, an alternative start for anyone using the steam railway as a means of getting about.

From the roadside parking area, cross the road with care and go through two gates opposite to follow a field-edge vehicle track. On the far side of the field, go forward through a metal kissing-gate and along the edge of the next field.

The field edge path leads up to the steam railway crossing at Colby Station. Over this, go forward along a surfaced lane to a crossroads. Cross into Colby Glen Road, noting the interesting village clock on the left.

Taking care against approaching traffic in the absence of footpaths, continue up the road as far as the gated and signposted turning into Colby Glen. Go down steps to the river and take either bank, the two paths meeting at the next bridge. Press on through delightful woodland to the third bridge (signpost) and there turn left to go up steps onto a narrow footpath flanked by bracken and leading into a hedgerowed path. Keep on to a kissing gate, and through it turn right along another hedged path that later opens out onto a broader farm track. Keep forward to a gate at a track junction. Turn left towards Cronkedooney, where the track joins a rough-surfaced lane and leads on to a lane corner.

Here, at a signpost, turn left and walk out to another junction opposite Ballakilpheric Methodist chapel. Go left and immediately right, passing a telephone box, Ballakilpheric Farm and, further on, the turning into Burn Brae, a large and conspicuous white house on the left. In the 1960s, this was just a small farmstead, but, like so many similar places on the island, has since been extensively renovated.

About 60m later, leave the lane at a signpost by turning left through a kissing-gate and alongside a metal fence towards Burn Brae. The way through the grounds of Burn Brae follows a pebble pathway and is way-marked as far as a ruined cottage (complete with interior bench) beside a kissing-gate.

Through the gate strike across the ensuing field to a hedge gap and then maintain the same direction in the next, towards some farm buildings (Scholaby Farm) and a metal gate, beside which there is a stone stile. Now

Ballacorkish Mine

Above the access lane descending from Scholaby Farm stands the chimney and ruins of the Ballacorkish Mine. This was one of the more successful of the island's mines and produced lead and zinc from three shafts, which reached a maximum depth of 140m (459ft). Work here ceased about 1895, when global competition made the mine unprofitable.

take to the ongoing farm access, a long, descending track that eventually reaches the end of a surfaced lane at Ballacorkish Farm. Continue down to reach a road junction, turn right and shortly go left at Level Garage into Croit e Caley.

Walk along the road, shortly crossing the line of the steam railway, passing Strawberry Fields and Strawberry Meadows, and continuing as far as a branching road on the right, with a footpath signpost nearby. Walk down to a metal gate, beside which there is a kissing-gate into a field. Bear left along the field edge to a corner hedge gap, and through this follow the left-hand edge of the next pasture to another kissing-gate. Maintain the same direction, now alongside a stream flanked by tall stands of rushes (fragmites).

Eventually the main coast road is reached near the Shore Hotel. Turn left, crossing the road with care, to follow the roadside footpath around the edge of the Bay ny Carrickey to return to the starting point.

WALK 29

Castletown and Scarlett Point

Distance:	5km (3 miles)
Map:	Isle of Man Outdoor Leisure Map: South
Start/Finish:	Scarlett, Castletown (grid ref 258666)
Parking:	Scarlett Point

With sea wind forever tussling your hair, even on the calmest days, this walk is invigorating and refreshing, providing scope for some useful seabird watching or the chance to lie back beside the path and watch Ronaldsway aircraft come and go. It's brevity leaves time for a full and proper exploration of Castletown, the former capital of the Isle of Man, and a place full of interest.

From the parking area walk along the coast, noting the nearby group of lime kilns down on the foreshore that are worth a quick inspection. They are linked with a water-filled quarry that soon appears on the right. Limestone was processed here and loaded onto ships at the nearby jetty.

Continue along the coast path passing first then **Scarlett Point** Visitor Centre and then the former coastguard lookout station (now home to an amateur radio club). Remain on the seaward side of a high wall. Gradually the wall becomes

Scarlett Point
The name derives from the Norse word, *skarfakluft*, meaning 'cormorant's cleft', a title still appropriate today – the rocks are favoured resting places not only of cormorants, but of shag, little auk, herring and black-backed gulls. Records show that Scarlett Point was one of the Norse 'Day Watch' hills, an early day coastguard lookout post.

dilapidated and starts losing its height. When the wall changes direction near some derelict buildings, you don't, but simply keep forward on a grassy path, passing the stony remains of a burial mound before pressing on to a ladder-stile spanning a wall.

Cross the next pasture and, in the third, follow the serpentine edge of an arable field. Keep going to reach a large earthwork, the remains of a small promontory fort with a ditch. Just beyond it another ladder stile gives on to a breakwater footpath at the edge of the **Poyllvaaish Quarry**.

Poyllvaaish Quarry
The rocks at Poyllvaaish have seen much volcanic activity and, as a result, have been metamorphosed at least three times. Although a limestone, the black beds of rock became known as Poyllvaaish Marble, which found its way into many of the grander homes on the island, into masons' factories to be fashioned in grave-stones and even to form the steps of St Paul's Cathedral in London. Alas, the rock weathers poorly, and while the steps of St Paul's had to be replaced, the grave-stones simply lost their inscriptions.

After passing the quarry a broad access track leads on, but follow it only as far as a signposted path on the right, heading across the edge of an arable field. Stay on the track as far as the next signpost, near an old gateway, and here leave the track by turning towards a concrete stile in a field corner. In the ensuing field go forward along the left-hand field edge alongside a drainage ditch. Over a ladder-stile keep in the same direction in the next field, passing stands of reeds to reach another ladder-stile.

Over the stile continue in the same direction, then follow the field edge round to a gap at an old gateway giving into the adjoining field. Turn into this and go round the edge of the field to a pill box. There cross a stile and turn right to another, and then head up the right-hand edge of the next field to a ladder-stile near a former windmill and Castle Rushen High School.

Behind the school turn right along an enclosed footpath ending at another ladder-stile. Go left here and follow the field edge, changing direction twice, to intercept a broad track flanked by low wall. This runs out to meet the Scarlett Point road. Turn right to return to the starting point.

Alternative finish: Over the ladder-stile at the rear of the high school, turn left and walk out to a road. Go through a kissing-gate and turn right, walking toward **Castletown** centre. On the edge of town, leave the main road and turn right onto Scarlett Road, passing rows of attractive cottages before finally breaking free of them and pressing on along the edge of Castletown Bay to return to the starting point.

Castletown

Castle Rushen dominates the ancient settlement of Castletown, the hub of Manx politics and power until Douglas assumed that role in the 19th century. The castle, a formidable structure, was home to many Manx kings, and was built largely during the 13th and 14th centuries, though some parts are older.

The town stands at the outflow of the Silverburn River, and many of the town's historic buildings are grouped around the harbour, notably the old grammar school, the oldest intact building on the island. In the days when Castletown was the capital, the island was governed from the House of Keys, now known as the 'Old' House of Keys, and recently restored to its former state so that visitors may see how the island was governed and learn something of its unique political system.

WALK 30
Silverdale Glen and Ballasalla

Distance:	7.5km (4¾ miles)
Map:	Isle of Man Outdoor Leisure Map: South
Start/Finish:	Silverdale Glen (grid ref 276710)
Parking:	At start
Refreshments:	Café and restaurant at start

Although one of the highlights of this walk is the opportunity to visit the historic Rushen Abbey, its real beauty lies in pastoral wandering across the farmlands south of Grenaby and the exquisite walking in the company of the Silver Burn through the lovely Silverdale Glen. The upper part of the glen is heady with the scent of wild garlic, bright with wild flowers and loud with birdsong. Here the Silver Burn fashions an enchanting course through a lightly wooded dale and the accompanying path cavorts along its flanks, sometimes close by the burn, at others high above it, but never far from its sight. The lower stretch of the glen is a little more 'managed'. Here, well-trodden footpaths lead beside the burn, past the Monks' Well to the Monks' Bridge and Rushen Abbey itself.

Silverdale Glen

Taking its name from the Silver Burn – the Awin Argid in Manx – which runs through it, Silverdale Glen is rightly one of the delights of the Manx countryside. Near the start an old watermill has been converted to a café and restaurant, with a boating lake and children's play area near by. One of the features here is a Victorian water-powered roundabout, with horses that date from the beginning of the 20th century. This is believed to be the only existing example of this type of roundabout in the world. The lower glen was given to the Manx National Trust in 1964 and contains a small well, the Monks' Well, just aside from the burn.

The walk begins from the restaurant and children's play area and boating lake on the site of an old watermill, between the upper and lower glens. Turn right out of the parking area and a few strides further on turn into the **Silverdale Glen**, almost immediately going left down to a burnside path. Take the path alongside the burn, but on the

Silverdale Glen

way through the glen, keep an eye open for the Monks' Well, just a few strides inland from the burn, but easily spotted.

The burnside path eventually leads out to a narrow gateway where it joins the Millennium Way. Here, turn left: the path wanders on, never far from the sight or sound of the burn, and in due course reaches the lovely double-arched Monks' Bridge.

From the bridge, continue forward along a surfaced lane. The lane comes out to meet a road adjoining Ye Olde Abbey Inn. On the left is a footbridge and a ford, and beyond that the centre of Ballasalla. But the route lies forward, passing the pub and soon reaching the entrance of **Rushen Abbey**.

Continue past the abbey to meet the main road. For safety's sake, cross the road with care to a memorial opposite, and turn right, but walk only as far as the next turning on the right (at a bad bend). Recross with care, ignore the road on the right, and turn instead up a stony track (signposted) that climbs briefly to a stone stile and kissing-gate at the rear of a couple of houses. Over the stile, go left along a field edge and soon divert left onto a path enclosed between low walls and hedgerows. At a gate with an unusual stile beside it, keep forward along a broad farm track leading to Ballahott Farm.

Pass through the farmyard and walk out to meet the Foxdale to Castletown road. Turn right, walking beside the road for about 275m, as far as the next turning on the left (signposted to Grenaby). Walk along the road until, just before a farm, you can branch left onto a sign-posted footpath, in the form of a surfaced lane. At the entrance to Ballavell Farm the surfacing ends and the track swings left, meandering across the countryside

Rushen Abbey

King Olaf I (known as Olaf the Dwarf) gave land for the founding of an abbey at Ballasalla in 1134, as a daughter house of Furness in Lancashire (as it then was). A date stone at the side of The Crossag, commemorates this date. This marked the beginning of the infiltration of monastic orders into island life. Like Furness, Rushen Abbey was originally of the Savignian (Benedictine) Order but it, too, in time became a Cistercian monastery. The grounds here contain the graves of three Viking kings of Mann who died between 1235 and 1265. The Cistercians were essentially manual workers, accepting neither tithes nor revenue, and proved to be outstanding 'farmers' as Rushen Abbey demonstrated, becoming by far the strongest force on the island, and the controller of all the best farm land: it also took charge of all mining and fishing and, with an abbot who was a baron in his own right, had the power of life and death.

The monks at Rushen Abbey were responsible for the earliest recorded history of the island, the *Chronicon Manniae*, which extended from the laying of the first foundation stone until 1374. Over the subsequent years, however, the abbey became less important, though its abbot and the last six brothers tenaciously held out against Henry VIII's dissolution of the monasteries longer than any other, being forcibly ejected in 1540.

*Monk's Bridge,
Rushen Abbey*

and flanked in spring and early summer by lady's smock, primrose, celandine, bluebell, yellow iris, wood sorrel, bugle and violet. Continue with the track until it forks and then bear right. When it next bends left (near a three-way signpost), leave it by turning right through a metal kissing-gate and walking up the right-hand edge of the ensuing field.

At the top of the field cross two stiles and, in the next field, turn right, following the field edge to the far corner to tackle two more stiles. Cross the end of the next field to another stile giving onto a wooden footbridge and, over this, keep to the right-hand of the next field to a gate giving onto a road. Now turn right and follow the road to a T-junction near the scattered hamlet of Grenaby.

Turn right for less than 100m and cross a ladder-stile on the left, then walk across the end of a field to a signpost at the top of a path descending towards the Silver Burn set in a woodland dell below.

The next stage of the walk roughly follows the course of the Silver Burn. It is a delight to follow, but has qualities that could prove taxing for young children: the route twists and turns, climbs and descends, is muddy and slippery in places, but never loses any of the magical quality that walking of this calibre brings.

A short way along the burn a stile gives onto a brief boggy stretch before finally descending to the banks of the burn. The burnside path eases along to a ladder-stile. Cross this and bear left to another stile, which gives, into a muddy corner from which you extricate yourself by bearing right before returning to a course parallel with and above the burn.

The path undulates across wooded slopes dominated by pungent wild garlic. When it eventually comes down to a small clearing with a new building and picnic table,

Tower, Rushen Abbey

go down steps onto a broad track leading out to the Foxdale to Castletown road. Cross with care and go onto the track opposite re-entering the Silverdale Glen and rejoining the Millennium Way.

Keep following an obvious path and when you reach the Silverdale Glen Mineral Water Factory cross a small bridge, passing to the right of the boating lake to return to the starting point.

119

WALK 31
Groudle Glen and Baldrine

Distance:	12km (7½ miles)
Map:	Isle of Man Outdoor Leisure Map: North
Start/Finish:	Groudle Glen (grid ref 420783)
Parking:	Groudle Glen
Refreshments:	Pub at Halfway House and in Baldrine

This lasso-shaped walk takes the opportunity to divert and visit the isolated St Lonan's Church and the magnificent wheel-headed cross in the graveyard. A measure of road walking makes for speedy progress, and does nothing to detract from the walk, which, in the main, passes through farming land.

From the parking area, cross a nearby footbridge and go up steps, part of the Raad ny Foillan. Follow the path up to reach and cross the **Groudle Glen** Railway line. Go forward on a continuing path, immediately passing a lime kiln.

Groudle Glen
Pronounced to rhyme with 'how', Groudle Glen is a neat, narrow nook on the boundary between Onchan and Lonan. Until 1962, the glen had a narrow gauge railway, opened in 1896 as a holiday attraction serving a number of entertainments in the glen. Work on reconstructing the railway began in 1982, and today it is fully restored and operated seasonally by a group of volunteers.

The route soon becomes a delightful, hedgerowed track ascending gently and flanked by sycamore, ivy and bluebells, and runs on to meet a surfaced lane. Keep forward and continue up the lane until you reach the turning to **St Lonan's Church**. Here, divert right on a side lane (signposted to St Adamnan's Church: Lonan Old Church) to visit the church, and then retrace the route and turn right onto the original line.

About 300m beyond the turning to St Lonan's Church, leave the road by turning left onto a signposted concrete track heading towards a farm. Follow this until it runs out to meet the Manx Electric Railway and then the A2. Turn left along the A2, and walk as far as the Liverpool Arms pub, there turning right onto a side road.

Continue up the lane to a signposted entrance to Harrison Farm/Bayr House and here turn right onto a rough track then almost immediately bear left onto a slightly narrower track, flanked by gorse. Continue following the track until it reaches a road on the edge of Baldrine and there turn right. Cross the electric railway again and go forward to a road junction. Turn left and walk downhill on a roadside footpath, then take the next turning on the right into Clay Head Road.

The Lonan Stone

This spectacular wheel-headed cross stands in the graveyard of Old Lonan Church, quite probably still in its original position, leaning gently to one side. It dates from the 9th or 10th century, and is by far the most attractive of the Manx crosses. The decoration consists entirely of Celtic interlacing, knots and plaits. The are other crosses in a small shelter within the churchyard.

St Lonan's Church

Curiously, this lovely old church isn't dedicated to St Lonan at all, but to St Adamnan, renowned biographer of St Columba, though he was also believed to be known by the name Onan. So, Lonan may be a corruption of Keeill Onan, the cell or chapel of Onan. Other authorities think the parish of Lonan is named after the third Bishop of Sodor and Man, a nephew of St Patrick, or that it was named after the Donegal saint, Lonan Machaisre.

Although part of the church is in ruins, the eastern end was restored at the end of the 19th century. The church is one of the island's oldest, some parts dating from the 12th century, and it stands on a site that was occupied by the earliest Christian missionaries. The first *keeill* was probably built on this site in the 5th century by travelling monks; it stood on the main packhorse route from Douglas to the north of the island. Originally, the chapel was known as Keeill-ny-Traie, the chapel by the shore, and served the surrounding quarterland farms at Baldromma, Ballacreggan, Ballameanagh, Ballavarane and the farm it stands on, Ballakilley. Almost certainly this early structure would have been destroyed by the Vikings and later re-built. In the 12th century, Reginald, King of Man, granted land at 'Escadalla', which included Keeill-ny-Traie, to the prior at St Bees in Cumberland. The monks there, having more than an eye for the main chance, quickly realised the importance of the chapel's location and rebuilt it to meet their needs. It is part of their building that now remains.

When the Vikings were finally vanquished at the Battle of Largs in 1263, the Isle of Man for a while belonged to Scotland, but soon passed to England. It was at this time that the parish system was introduced to the island and Keeill-ny-Traie became the parish church, dedicated to St Adamnan. And so it remained until the 18th century, when the parishioners complained about the church's inconvenient location at the southern edge of their parish. It took 100 years before a new church was finally built at Boilley Veen, although this, too, was remote. The Act of Tynwald sanctioning the building of the new church also required the demolition of the old one; an instruction that, thankfully, was ignored; even so, the old church fell into disrepair. That part of the church is in serviceable condition today is largely thanks to the Reverend John Quinne, vicar of Lonan from 1895, who initiated the restoration of the church.

Keep following the lane and reach a double gate at the entrance to Clay Head Farm. Go through this and continue walking for about 50m and then turn right on a signposted footpath over a concrete stile beside a gate. Stay along the right-hand edge of the ensuing field to reach a ladder-stile. Over this bear left along an enclosed track. Keep following the track which eventually finds a way round to a group of farm buildings at the Ballannetts Conservation Nature Reserve, Wildlife and Wetlands Area, and then continue beyond it on a concrete vehicle track, heading towards a group of lakes.

Eventually the track comes out onto a lane. Turn left and soon rejoin the outward route of the walk near St Lonan's Church. Now retrace your steps back to the start in Groudle Glen.

Wheelhead cross,
St Lonan's Church

WALK 32
Baldwin, Union Mills and Crosby

Distance:	13km (8 miles)
Map:	Isle of Man Outdoor Leisure Map: South
Start/Finish:	Crosby (grid ref 326795)
Parking:	Roadside parking at Crosby
Refreshments:	Crosby, Union Mills

Visiting three ancient settlements, this tour of the farm-lands north of the River Dhoo begins along a stretch of the Millennium Way and then uses fields to reach Baldwin, before making good use of old lanes to return to Union Mills from where the old Douglas to Peel railway trackbed provides an easy means of return to Crosby.

After parking considerately in Old Church Road in Crosby, walk back to the main road and cross into Eyreton Road. The route is signposted as part of the Millennium Way, which indeed it is, as far as Baldwin.

Continue up the lane until it swings to the right, and here leave it by going forward onto a rough stony track between walls. In the field on the left note the fenced site of St Bridget's Chapel (Keeill Vreeshey). Carry on up the lane to a junction and there turn left for a little over 100m to a Millennium Way signpost, leaving the lane at a kissing-gate for a field-edge path.

Keep to the field edge and follow this to a through-stile (signpost). Over this, go forward along another field edge, but then leaving the field after about 100m, by bearing right over another stile. In the ensuing pasture, again keep to the field headland, following this round to a stile beside a signpost. A large pasture now follows. Keep forward along the left-hand edge. At a gate on the far side of the field, go through onto a farm access.

The track runs on to the edge of Ballalough Farm. Here go forward to a footpath signpost and turn left, over a stile and kissing-gate (old Millennium waymarker just over the stile). Continue along the field edge to stiles spanning an electrified fence, one either side of a field track. Now go straight across the next pasture to cross another electrified fence, a track and ladder-stile.

Cross another field and on the other side turn right towards Ballagrawe, from where its access leads downhill to Annie's Cottage (signposted 'Millennium Way FP152') and a right turn towards Baldwin, finally meeting the village road at a T-junction.

Turn right for 200m and then leave the main road for an ascending lane on the right (bridleway signpost). Follow the lane past The Rhyne and, a short way further on, leave

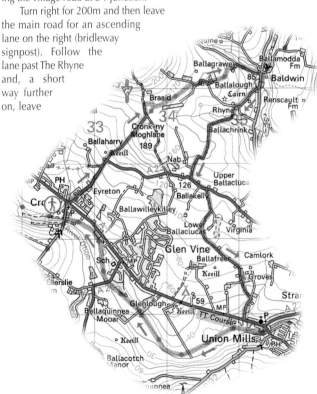

the surfaced lane by turning left at a signpost onto another stony track flanked by overgrown walls.

The descending track treks between farm fields for some distance before finally coming down to meet a road. Turn left and, after about 300m, turn right at a signposted lane between established hedgerows of gorse and hawthorn. After 350m bear right towards a metal gate, continuing on a hedgerowed lane (Trollaby Lane). Keep on down the lane to meet the main road, and there turn left towards Union Mills.

Just by the Shell garage, cross the road with care and, just before the bridge spanning the River Dhoo, turn right into a small industrial estate at the far side of which a gate gives onto the trackbed of the Douglas to Peel railway line. Turn right onto this and now follow the trackbed, part of the Heritage Trail, for 4km (2½ miles), crossing the road up to Glen Vine at a derelict gatehouse and continuing, the trackbed now surfaced, to the next gatehouse near the site of the former Crosby Station. Here turn right to return to the start. The trackbed passes through an extensive area of wetland (known as curragh), which is a good place to keep an eye open for birdlife and wild flowers.

WALK 33
Slieau Ruy and Greeba Mountain

Distance:	11km (6¾ miles)
Map:	Isle of Man Outdoor Leisure Map: South
Start/Finish:	Crosby (grid ref 326795)
Parking:	Roadside parking at Crosby
Refreshments:	Crosby, Union Mills

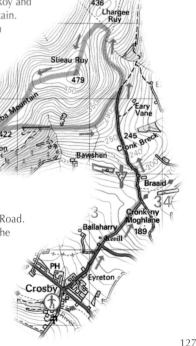

The first part of this walk follows Walk 32, using a section of the Millennium Way before bearing off to climb onto Slieau Ruy and its lower satellite, Greeba Mountain. Although both summits lie within the Area of Public Ramblage, they are not often visited and the terrain is potentially confusing, making this walk unsuitable for days of poor visibility.

There is plenty of room to park tidily in Old Church Road in Crosby, and from here walk out to the main road, crossing with care into Eyreton Road. The route is signposted as part of the Millennium Way.

Continue up the lane until it swings to the right, and here leave it by going forward onto a rough stony track between walls. In the field on the left note the fenced site of

St Bridget's Chapel (Keeill Vreeshey). Carry on up the lane to a junction, and there turn left.

Shortly, leave the Millennium Way (which crosses into an adjacent field) and keep forward to pass Braaid Farm, beyond which the lane becomes steeper and quite rough underfoot. Go past the turning to Bawshen and continue uphill (signposted for Little London), eventually passing the track down to the ruins of Eary Vane Farm. At a cattle grid the route reaches the edge of an area of public ramblage, and continues roughly northwards, but bearing left to cross the top of a stream gully. Slieau Ruy now lies to the south-west.

Keep on to a path junction (signpost for Rhenass) and there turn abruptly left heading for the summit of Slieau Ruy, the top of which is marked by a trig pillar and cairn. There is an outstanding view from the summit, and the surprise is that the hill is not more popular.

Continue now by following the lie of the land as you head for Greeba Mountain (it is not a direct line, though one is possible). By keeping to the highest ground between the two summits, albeit boggy at some times of year, the top of Greeba Mountain is soon reached. Fine views also await here, for this is one of the best vantage points on the island.

From the top of Greeba Mountain head eastwards to intercept a wall at the top boundary of Greeba Plantation, then maintain an easterly direction along the plantation boundary to reach a stream at its easterly edge. Cross the stream and now contour east and north-east, following a wall along the boundary of the Area of Public Ramblage. This leads back to the cattle grid crossed on the outward leg. Here turn right and retrace the walk back to Crosby.

Anyone wanting a really long walk, and quite a demanding one too, should consider linking this walk with that to Baldwin and Union Mills (Walk 32) to give a walk of 20km (12½ miles).

WALK 34

Port Grenaugh, Port Soldrick and Cass ny Hawin

Distance:	5km (3 miles)
Map:	Isle of Man Outdoor Leisure Map: South
Start/Finish:	Port Grenaugh (grid ref 316706)
Parking:	Port Grenaugh

It isn't long before the thoughts of anyone wandering the coastal cliffs of the island turn to the history of smuggling, a trade in which the islanders were key players. Along this walk we pass Jackdaw Cave, just at the entrance to Port Soldrick, which was a hideaway much favoured by smugglers.

From the road end at Port Grenaugh turn right across a footbridge to follow the Raad ny Foillan along the edge of the pebbly beach to gain a rising path on the other side, climbing onto the headland.

Continue following the coastal path, which occasionally moves into adjacent fields, and back again, and then finds a way to and around Port Soldrick. The coastal scenery is outstanding and popular with birds, notably chough, which often gather in flocks, gulls, fulmars and cormorants, which adopt affected poses on water's edge rocks.

Gradually, the path moves round to meet the narrow and long inlet of Cass ny Hawin, where the Santon Burn flows into the sea. Dense stands of gorse fill the air with the heady scent of coconut, cinnamon or nutmeg (according to nasal sensitivities – we all seem to identify different things). Through the gorse, the path steadily works a way upstream.

Confronted with a choice of turning right into a field or going left down towards the burn, turn left. The path accompanying the burn is a delight to follow, if a little muddy, and leads to a bridge spanning the burn, where the coastal path goes left. Here, keep forward on a broad grassy track. A short way further on it joins a rutted vehicle track. Turn left along this, which in turn leads out to a surfaced lane.

Turn up the lane, keeping an eye open for a prominent hut circle mound topped with rocks in a field on the left. Remain on the lane until about 100m after a derelict cottage on the right, you can turn right on a road to Ballafurt. Go down past Ballafurt Cottage and past a metal gate to a ladder-stile giving into a large field. Keep to the left-hand edge of the field until you can switch sides into an adjacent field, now following the right-hand edge to rejoin the coastal path at a kissing-gate. Now simply turn left and retrace your outward route back to Port Grenaugh.

Jackdaw Cave
Just at the entrance to Port Soldrick a fine sea cave appears on the east side of the cove. This is Jackdaw Cave, a genuine smuggler's hideout into which boats would sail, to be loaded via a hole in the roof of the cave.

WALK 35

Port Grenaugh, Pistol Bay and Santon Head

Distance:	7km (4½ miles)
Map:	Isle of Man Outdoor Leisure Map: South
Start/Finish:	Port Grenaugh (grid ref 316706)
Parking:	Port Grenaugh

Port Grenaugh is a rarely visited nook tucked away on the south coast of the island. Following a good section of the coastal path, the walk begins by heading across country before turning for the sea.

From the end of the road turn left through an ornate kissing gate onto a narrow path, rising beside a stream, and soon crossing the stream twice in quick succession as a gravel path leads you up through an attractively cultivated interlude to another kissing gate. Through this turn

Near the start of the Port Grenaugh walk

131

left and follow a broad track to another gate adjacent to Arragon House. Go forward past the house to a T-junction, and turn right.

Go across a cattle grid and keep forward on a broad vehicle track. Go as far as a gate and cross a stile beside it, and another stile a short way ahead, now striding along a broad grassy path between gorse banks.

At the next set of gates, turn left onto a dirt track (following the course of overhead electricity powerlines).

Looking back to the cliffs of Pistol Bay

The track rises to meet a concrete road. Turn left and continue following the road until you reach a crossroads, where the track intercepts the Raad ny Foillan (the coastal path).

Turn right, climbing gently along a surfaced lane flanked by gorse embankments, vivid with colour in spring and early summer. Continue until the road levels and then leave it by turning right at a signposted footpath on the right, crossing a stone step-stile to head down a broad vehicle track to a ladder-stile beside a gate. Over this, go forward alongside a gorse hedge on the left, finally rising to a gate in a field corner. Through this turn right for a sudden and stunning view of the coast, especially to the left where the crags of Pistol Castle put on a fine display.

The path soon descends through gorse which at some times of year can partially obscure the path, which is narrow and often close to the cliff edge. The gorse can take its toll of bare legs, too, but is interspersed with grassy oases on which it is delightful to sit and watch the birds that frequent the rocks below – cormorants, chough, fulmar, herring gull. Sea thrift grows everywhere, along with squill, scarlet pimpernel and celandine, while most of the walls display a healthy mantle of mosses.

Continue following the coastal path through all its twists and turns, ups and downs, heading towards the conspicuous inlet of Grenaugh Cove. Just before reaching it, a huge dome on the left of the path alerts you to something intriguing. This is **Cronk ny Merriu**, beyond which the path descends to the road end.

Cronk ny Merriu

Occupying a prominent position along the south coast, Cronk ny Merriu is a fortified promontory fort with defensive ditch and rampart. The defences were probably Iron Age or from the first few centuries AD. There are also the foundations of a Viking house (10th–11th century) within the fort. It was this period of occupation that gave the cove its name: Port Grenaugh is Norse for 'green creek'.

WALK 36

*St John's, Slieau Whallian,
Patrick and the Heritage Trail*

Distance:	11.5km (7 miles)
Map:	Isle of Man Outdoor Leisure Map: South
Start/Finish:	St John's (grid ref 277817)
Parking:	Car park at old railway station, opposite St John's Primary School
Refreshments:	Two pubs in St John's

This walk combines ancient routes of different kinds – railway and trade – but its real purpose is to wander across the gorse-decked flanks of Slieau Whallian. It begins not far from Tynwald Hill, to which everyone should make a short detour to visit the museum and the Royal Chapel of St John the Baptist. Once free of the Slieau Whallian Plantation, the route romps up to cross the south-western shoulder of the hill before plunging down to Kirk Patrick. The return is along a stretch of the Heritage Trail, the reincarnation of the

Royal Chapel of St John the Baptist

Not only is the church the parish church of the village of St John's, it is also the National Civic Church for the island, the 'Tynwald Church'. On Tynwald Day the church performs two functions. It is, of course, the consecrated building used for the religious element of the day, but later it also acts as a court house. The present church was built by Richard and Benjamin Lane of Manchester in the 13th-century style known as English Transitional. It is faced with granite from South Barrule quarry, but also uses stone from Ballavar, with chancel steps in Poyllvaaish marble.

Little is known about the early history of this site, but it is probable that there has been a place of worship here or hereabouts since the 10th century. Evidence for this comes in the form of a runic cross – Osruth's Cross – dating from AD 950 and unearthed when the 1699 cross-shaped church was demolished in 1847. The cross stands in the porch of the present church.

route of the now defunct Isle of Man Railway between Douglas and Peel.

Opposite the entrance to the new primary school in St John's is the surfaced entrance to a car park at what was the old railway station. From here walk out to the road and turn right to pass the Farmers' Arms pub and shortly turn right again, into Patrick Road. Then, immediately after a road bridge spanning a burn, turn left into a rising lane signposted to Gleneedle.

Walk up the road as far as a gate and stile on the right-hand side, giving entrance to the Slieau Whallian Plantation. An agreeable track ascends steadily through the plantation, but is short-lived and

Tynwald Hill, St John's

Tynwald Hill

Said to be composed of earth gathered from the 17 parishes on the island, and so representing the whole island, Tynwald Hill is a man-made four-tiered mound adjoining the road at St John's, and the focal point of the island's legislature, representing, as it does, an unbroken tradition of a parliamentary assembly in the Isle of Man more than a thousand years old. There is some suggestion that the site of Tynwald Hill marks the spot of an ancient burial mound.

The name 'Tynwald' is derived from the Norse language, in which a *thing* is an assembly or meeting, and *vollr*, a field. The original principles of the ancient *Thing-vollr* are still the basis of the Manx constitution today. Normally, the Court of Tynwald meets throughout the year in Douglas, but annually, on the Old Midsummer's Day (5th July), the monarch (represented by the Lieutenant-Governor), the High Court Judges (known as Deemsters), the elected members of the House of Keys (the Lower House and the equivalent of the British House of Commons), the appointed members of the Legislative Council (the Upper House), and a number of civic authorities meet to give effect to the island's laws, proclaiming them in both English and Manx. The occasion is the only time in the year when the West Door of St John's Church is opened, to access the processional way that leads directly from the church to Tynwald Hill, a distance of 110m.

St John's is not unique in having an outdoor Tynwald: others have been held at Cronk Urleigh, near Kirk Michael, and at Cronk Keeill Abban, near St Luke's Church north of Baldwin.

finally emerges at another gate. Beyond lies a walled track that skirts the top of Slieau Whallian, crosses its shoulder and then descends to a road corner. Other than to touch on it briefly, the road plays no part in this walk. Instead, turn right onto another walled track which leads unerringly down to meet the Kirk Patrick to St John's road not far from the church in Kirk Patrick. Turn left towards the church, and go past it to a T-junction, there turning right, towards Peel.

After about 1km (⅔ mile) the road dinks across a road bridge. Just as you cross the bridge, turn right down wooden steps to meet the River Neb near an old watermill. Here you have joined the Heritage Trail, and the old trackbed can be followed, right, for about 4km (2½ miles) back to a couple of gates giving into the car parking area on the site of the old St John's Station.

WALK 37

Glen Maye and the Postman's Path

Distance:	1.5km (1 mile)
Map:	Isle of Man Outdoor Leisure Map: South
Start/Finish:	Glen Maye (grid ref 236798)
Parking:	Opposite Waterfall Hotel
Refreshments:	Waterfall Hotel

Glen Maye means the 'yellow glen' and a walk through it in spring and early summer amply shows why: gorse bushes cover the glen sides and the farmland above bringing a vivid golden hue to the landscape.

The descent into Glen Maye requires no description. The path is clear and obvious all the way as far as the remains of a waterwheel, passing through woodland that is alive in springtime with birdsong and bright with the colour of wild flowers. From the waterwheel you have three possibilities: retrace your steps through the glen; walk out to the nearby road and either go left to walk down to the seashore, or turn right to walk back up the road to the Waterfall Hotel. (The distance to the seashore and back is about 2km/1½ miles, and should be added if you are doing both halves of this short walk.)

To tie in with the Postman's Path, leave the car park and turn left into the village, going up Hillside Terrace and, before reaching the post office, turn right onto a side lane that ultimately leads through to Glen Rushen. Follow this beyond the last houses, where a

In Glen Maye

wooden barrier prevents further use by cars. For pedestrians the old glen road, gradually becoming overgrown, is a delight. Follow it until you reach a waymarked path descending on the right above the Glen Maye River.

The path gradually descends to reach the riverbank and then crosses it at a footbridge. Over the bridge bear right through gorse – keep an eye open for grey heron's that like to feed in this sheltered spot. At a signpost turn left onto a broad track (the Postman's Path) leading out to a lane. There turn right and walk out to join the Glen Maye to Dalby road, once more bearing right to walk back up to the Waterfall Hotel.

WALK 38

Derbyhaven, St Michael's Island and Langness

Distance:	variable up to 8km (5 miles)
Map:	Isle of Man Outdoor Leisure Map: South
Start/Finish:	Derbyhaven (grid ref 284676)
Parking:	Derbyhaven
Refreshments:	Derbyhaven

This is a walk with no set route description, but it would be quite unthinkable to produce a book of walks to the Isle of Man without suggesting an exploration of the peninsula of Langness and adjacent St Michael's Island. It is possible to drive to a parking area at grid ref 284660 and this will avoid having to walk across a golf course, but there is a good surfaced road across the course, and on a fine, sunny day the whole of this isolated part of the island can consume far more time than the distance involved might suggest. Take a picnic and perch among the rocks of Langness Point if it's serious chilling out you're in search of.

Derbyhaven is a neat gathering of houses and cottages built on the neck of land between Castletown Bay and the bay of Derby Haven. A road runs south from the village around the southern edge of Derby Haven, passing a

Derbyhaven

Once the island's chief fishing port, Derbyhaven was the port of the Derby family, established by the 2nd Earl, Thomas III, in 1507. During the time of the Norsemen, the place was known as Rognvald's Vagir, or Ronald's Way – the name now given to the island's airport – and, like the airport, saw many landings on the island. The port was the scene, in 1275, of a battle in which John de Vesci, agent of Alexander of Scotland, having failed to negotiate with the Manxmen over the question of Scottish rule of the island, slaughtered over 500 men and brought their revolt to an end.

St Michael's Island

large golfing hotel and continues across a causeway – strong winds and a high tide are good times to avoid, if you don't want a drenching here – onto St Michael's Island. The island is a small grassy appendage but contains Derby Fort, a round fortification, along with the ruins of St Michael's Chapel.

Return back towards Derbyhaven, but before reaching the first houses, take a road on the left which curves back southwards and heads across the golf course. The rocks of Castletown Bay are a good place to look for birdlife, while, further out, you may spot the occasional seal or harbour porpoise.

Go down as far as the parking area, where you can leave the surfaced road, and bear right to follow

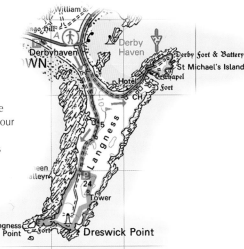

Langness
The long peninsula of Langness has a splendid coastline of rocks and caves, and has at its extreme point a reef called the Skerranes, where many a ship has come to grief. The prominent cylindrical tower was built in 1816 as a landmark for shipping before the building of the lighthouse, and is known locally as the Herring Tower.

*Round Tower,
Langness*

the edge of Castletown Bay out to Langness Point. Head back round towards Dreswick Point and the lighthouse, the last lighthouse on the island to be automated.

Continue now up the eastern coastline, passing the Round Tower, shortly after which you need to turn left alongside a wall to return to the parking area, and the road back out across the golf course.

WALK 39

Mull Hill, Spanish Head and The Chasms

Distance:	7km (4⅓ miles)
Map:	Isle of Man Outdoor Leisure Map: South
Start/Finish:	Port Erin (grid ref 196689)
Parking:	Port Erin
Refreshments:	Port Erin, Cregneash (seasonal), The Sound (off-route)

I had long looked at the tangle of footpaths that radiate from Cregneash with a view to sorting out a walk across the middle of this southern bit of the island, but always been distracted by the stunning coastal route between Port St Mary and Port Erin. As my weeks on the island came to a close, I finally succumbed, on the very last day, foregoing a moorland tramp north of Baldwin for the pathways of Rushen: and I was mightily glad that I did, because it turned out to be superb even though it had parts in common with other walks.

Begin from the sea front in Port Erin and walk towards the Bay Hotel, immediately beyond which a surfaced pathway on the left rises to reach a large house, now converted to apartments. Walk round this and turn up the access driveway to meet a rough lane fronting more houses (Darrag). From this point there is a lovely retrospective view over Port Erin to Bradda Hill and Lhiattee ny Beinnee.

Turn left and walk out to a surfaced lane, meeting it at a bend. Turn right, ascending, and keep going until the gradient eases and you reach a largish grassy lay-by on the left-hand side of the road. Up above you, you

The Chasms

Cregneash fields
The fields close to Cregneash village are now being farmed with methods used in the area from about 1890. Clydesdale horses provide the main motive power. Oats, barley, potatoes, swedes and vegetables like cabbages and carrots can be seen growing together with flax for linen and fibre. Because straw is needed for thatching, wheat is grown although it is not traditional in this area. Most of the holdings in the village were crofts of between 6 and 8 acres (roughly 2–4ha), each supporting two or three cows and some poultry.

can see a fenced area. Take the footpath that leads up to this and, over a step-stile, enter the grounds of the Meayll Stone Circle.

Go across another stile at the back, and walk onto the top of Mull Hill, site of a Second World War radar station. Continue through this to locate a prominent and descending broad gravel track that curves back down to the single track road. Turn left onto the road and left again to head for Cregneash village. When a branching lane into the village appears, go down this, and keep forward to reach the last thatched cottage on the right (Harry Kelly's Cottage). Turn right here to locate the start of the Church Farm Walk.

Turn left, along a walled track, and follow this until the track forks at Spanish Head Road. Here, keep forward, branching left at a signpost. The track twists and turns, flanked by overgrown walls and gorse, and the route is waymarked when it needs to be. It leads eventually to a boardwalk section before curving round to face The Chasms – a spectacular moment.

The path finally descends to intercept the coastal path. Go left along it, heading for The Chasms, and climbing steadily to an isolated building that was once a café. Just past it, bear right through a fence (signpost) and walk down beside a wall to a step-stile across which you can get a good view of Sugar Loaf and the cliffs of The Chasms. But the route does not cross the stile. Instead, from it, bear left down to a gate and stone stile and, over this, head down to a signpost at the end of a walled lane heading for Port St Mary.

Enter the walled lane, and keep going until in due course it becomes surfaced as the first houses are reached. A short way on, where the lane forks, branch left for The Howe and Port Erin, into Glen Chass.

Continue through Glen Chass and, on the far side, meet the Cregneash road. Turn left, up the road, for about 150m, to a signpost on the right (take the first of two) and here leave the road for a track passing to the left of a barn. When the track reaches a derelict cottage, go ahead over a stile onto a path that leads across fields to emerge near a white cottage at a stile.

Turn onto a signposted track, past the cottage and maintaining height across the hillside, heading for a signpost and stile in a wall corner near three gates. Cross the stile and, in the ensuing field, shortly bear left through gorse to another stone stile. Over this, go forward alongside a fence to another stile beside a gate and pass through a nearby kissing-gate onto a wallside path, targeting the tower on Bradda Head. Soon the route reaches a small group of stiles and footpath signposts. Here, over the last of these, beside a metal gate, bear right, down a grassy track between hedgerows.

Continue down to meet a road. Cross this and go forward on a surfaced pathway leading into an estate road. Keep forward to another pathway to the right of a house opposite. This leads into a cul-de-sac. Bear left along another path to pass more houses and walk out to a road junction. Turn left to another junction near by, and go forward into Athol Park. At the far end of Athol Park, swing right to a main road junction and there turn left to go down to the seafront.

WALK 40

South Barrule

Distance:	2km (1¼ miles)
Map:	Isle of Man Outdoor Leisure Map: South
Start/Finish:	Round Table (grid ref 247757)
Parking:	At junction of Bayr ny Skeddan and Dalby road

This brief walk is for those who simply want to 'conquer' South Barrule, one of the principal summits on the island, a Marilyn for those who believe in such things, but most importantly an important prehistoric site with an impressive hill fort.

There is a limited amount of parking space where the Bayr ny Skeddan emerges from Corlea Plantation and meets the main road near **Round Table**. Here a kissing-gate gives onto a path through heather that climbs unerringly to the

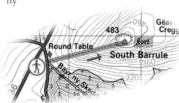

Round Table
Thoughts that the Round Table might have some association with King Arthur and his knights should be instantly dispelled. The answer lies in an insignificant heather-topped mound between the start of this walk and the crossroads nearby. It lies just over the wall on the parish boundary, a small tumulus of significance unknown, but, being called the 'Round Table' is said to be the place where the watchers on the summit would gather to take their meals – an unlikely story, of course.

summit of South Barrule. It requires no description, and is neither steep nor overlong, little more than 1km (⅔ mile), in fact.

Details of the summit hill fort are contained in Walk 18: it is a fine vantage point and takes in most of the southern part of the island, a distinction that made it one of the 'early warning' Watch Hills during the Norse occupation of the island.

From the summit, simply go back the way you came. Walk 22 contains an extended walk across the summit and down the other side.

The shapely summit of South Barrule

APPENDIX A
Longer Waymarked Walks

The **Millennium Way** was the first long distance path to be created on the Isle of Man, to coincide with the Millennium Year of the Tynwald, in 1979. The route is based on the Royal Way to Ramsey, the 'Via Regia' first chronicled in the 14th century. It starts from Castle Rushen in Castletown and passes through Ballasalla, Silverdale Glen, Crosby and Baldwin before reaching Ramsey, a distance of 45km (28 miles), well within the day capabilities of experienced long distance walkers, but also easily adapted to a two- or three-day itinerary using public transport at the end of each day. The final stage from Baldwin is across open moorland requiring walkers to be fully equipped for all eventualities.

Raad ny Foillan (The Road of the Gull) runs around the coast of the island and embraces some truly spectacular scenery on the way. It is 153km (95 miles) of superb walking, not too demanding, and do-able easily in eight days. The Raad ny Foillan was opened in 1986 to mark the island's Heritage Year, but the idea of a coastal footpath was mooted much earlier, by Sir Ambrose Dundas Flux Dundas, a former governor of the island and enthusiastic rambler.

The coastline of the island is rightly regarded as a national treasure by the Manx, so you'll encounter little that detracts from its natural beauty. The route follows the coastline as much as possible from the shingle beaches at the northern end of the island to 180m (591ft) high hills and cliffs above the Sloc.

Bayr ny Skeddan (The Herring Road) is based on a route taken by the Manx fishermen as they journeyed between Castletown and Peel. Weighing in at a mere 23km (14¼ miles), this is a walk that most fit walkers can complete easily in a day.

Initially following the Millennium Way, the Bayr ny Skeddan heads north after Silverdale Glen and strikes across the moorland divide near the Round Table and South Barrule. It then heads for Glen Maye where it meets up with the Raad ny Foillan for the final leg into Peel.

The **Heritage Trail** runs for a modest 17km (10½ miles) from the outskirts of Douglas, using the route of the now defunct Isle of Man Railway Company's lines to Peel.

APPENDIX B

Useful Addresses and Organisations

Isle of Man Tourism

Sea Terminal Buildings
Douglas
Isle of Man
IM1 2RG
Tel: (Info) 01624 686766
            (General) 01624 686801
Fax: 01624 686800
Email: tourism@gov.im
Internet: www.visitisleofman.com

Manx National Heritage

Manx Museum
Douglas
Isle of Man
IM1 3LY
Tel: 01624 648000
Fax: 01624 648001

Tourist Information Offices

(some seasonal):

Airport	Tel: 01624 821600
Castletown	Tel: 01624 825005
Port St Mary	Tel: 01624 832101
Port Erin	Tel: 01624 832298
Peel	Tel: 01624 842341
Ramsey	Tel: 01624 817025
Onchan	Tel: 01624 621228
Ballasalla	Tel: 01624 822531

APPENDIX C
Bibliography

Ancient and Historic Monuments, The
(Manx National Heritage, 4th edition, 1973)

Clucas, S. D. *The Thousla Cross*

Cubbon, A. M. *The Art of the Manx Crosses*
(Manx National Heritage, 3rd edition, 1983)

Evans, Aileen *Isle of Man Coastal Path* (Cicerone Press, 1988 and 1991).

Freeman, T. W. et al *Lancashire, Cheshire and the Isle of Man*
(Thomas Nelson, 1966)

Kneale, Trevor *The Isle of Man* (Pevensey Island Guide, 2001)

Prehistoric Sites in the Isle of Man
(Manx National Heritage, 4th impression, 1986)

Rimington, John *Features and History of the Meayll Peninsula*
(Rushen Parish Commissioners, 2000)

The Royal Chapel of St John the Baptist: A Short History and Guide to 'The Tynwald Church'

Salter, Mike *Castles and Old Churches of the Isle of Man*
(Folly Publications, 1997)

Stenning, E. H. *Portrait of the Isle of Man*
(Robert Hale, 1958, 1965, 1975 and 1978)

Young, G. V. C. *A Brief History of the Isle of Man*
(Mansk-Svenska Publishing, Peel, 2nd edition, 1999)

APPENDIX D

Glossary of Manx Terms and Place Names

Most of the place names found on the Isle of Man have Gaelic origins and serve as a reminder that the Manx Gaelic language was once widely spoken here. Other names are of Norse origin, especially those that refer to coastal features. Places like Foxdale have been Anglicised, in this case from *fors dala*, waterfall dale. Elsewhere, you'll find names that are distinctly English, and a few that distinctly are not.

a	river (as in Laxa, Cornaa, Rumsa, Crogga)	glion	glen
		gob	point, promontory
ard	height	howe	headland
ayre	gravel beach	keeill	chapel
balla	farm, place (of)	kerroo	quarterland
beg, veg	little	knock	hillock
broogh	bank, brow	lag, laggan	hollow
byr, by	homestead (as in Crosby)	logh	lake
		mooar, vooar	great, big
cashtal	castle	pooyl	pool
claddagh	river meadow	purt, phurt	port, harbour
creg, creggan	rock	reeast	moorland
croit	croft	sallagh	willow
cronk	hill	slieau	mountain
curragh	marsh, bogland	spooyt	waterfall
fell	mountain (as in Sartfell)	stakkr	sea stack
garroo	rough	vik	creek

Some Manx Place Names

Agneash (Scand)	eggjornes (edge ness); ness (nose/promontory)
Arragon (Old Irish)	O'Rogan's river-mouth
Baldwin (Scand)	bol (homestead); (dalr) dale
Baldromma (Manx)	balla (farm/place of); drommey (ridge)
Ballacallin (Manx)	balla (farm/place of); macallyn – callin
Ballacreggan (Manx)	balla (farm/place of); creggan (stones)
Ballachurry (Manx)	balla (farm/place of); churry/charry (mire/dung)

Ballacuberagh (Manx)	balla (farm/place of); Coobragh – Cuthbert
Ballacurnkeil (Manx)	balla (farm/place of); curn (Curry's); keil (of the church)
Ballfurt (Manx)	balla (farm/place of); phurt (port/harbour)
Ballaglass (Manx)	balla (farm/place of); glass (green – green farm)
Ballagrawe (Manx)	balla (farm/place of); ny (of the); gro (acorns)
Ballakilley (Manx)	balla (farm/place of); keeil (church)
Ballakilpheric (Manx)	balla (farm/place of); keeil (church); Pheric (Patrick)
Ballameanagh (Manx)	balla (farm/place of); meanagh (middle)
Ballaragh (Manx)	balla (farm/place of); arraght (ghost)
Ballasalla (Manx)	balla (farm/place of); sallagh (sallies – reeds/rushes)
Ballaugh/Ballalough (Manx)	balley ny loughy (place of the lake/lough)
Ballavarane (Manx)	balla (farm/place of); Verane (obsolete Irish name)
Ballavell (Manx)	balla (farm/place of); vell (corruption of Bell – Bell's farm)
Ballayolgane (Manx)	balley (farm/place of); yolgane (Golgane's – old Irish surname)
Balleira (Manx)	balla (farm/place of); leira (muddy stream)
Bay ny Carricky (Manx)	bay ny (bay of); carricky (stones)
Bayr Glass (Manx)	bayr (road); glass (green – green road)
Block Eary (Scand)	block (black); eary (sheiling)
Bradda (Norse)	bratthaugr (steep headland)
Carn Vael (Manx)	carn (cairn); Vael (Michael – Michael's cairn)
Carrick(ey) (Manx)	a sea-rock (Carrick Rock – a sea-rock rock!)
Cashtel Mooar (Manx)	cashtel (castle); mooar/vooar (big)
Cass ny Hawin (Manx)	cass (fort); ny (of the); hawin (river)
Clagh Ouyr (Manx)	clagh (stone); ouyr (dunn coloured – brown stone)
Close ny Chollagh (Manx)	close (enclosure); ny (of the); chollagh (stallions)
Colby (Scand)	col (Kolli's); byr (farm)
Cooildarry (Manx)	cooil (hidden place); darrag (bog oaks)
Corlea (Manx)	cor (hill); lleagh (grey)
Cregneash (Manx)	creg (rock); ny (of); eash (ages)
Cregneash (Scand)	krakurness (promontory of the crows)
Cronkedooney (Manx)	cronk (hill); e (of the); Dooney (The Lord's Day – Sunday)

Cronk Keeil Abbon (Manx)	cronk (hill); keeil (church); Abbon (saint's name)
Cronk Koir (Manx)	cronk (hill); koir (storage chest – sometimes 'kist')
Cronk Moar (Manx)	cronk (hill); moar/mooar (big)
Cronk ny Arrey Laa (Manx)	cronk (hill); ny (of the); arrey-laa (day-watch; laa – day)
Cronk ny Irree Laa (Manx)	cronk (hill); ny (of the); irree-laa (day-break)
Cronk ny Merriu (Manx)	cronk (hill); ny (of the); marroo (dead)
Cronk Shamerk (Manx/Scand)	cronk (hill); shamerk – skammhyggr (short ridge)
Cronk Sumark (Manx)	cronk (hill); sumark (primrose)
Cronk Urleigh (Manx)	cronk (hill); urleigh (slaughter (now 'eagle'), by default from the damage caused to the sheep flocks by 'eagles' (though none ever recorded on the island)
Crosby (Scand)	kros (cross); byr (farm)
Dalby (Scand)	dal-byr (dale-farm)
Dreswick (Scand)	drangsvik (rock creek)
Eary Cushlin (Manx)	eary (sheiling); cushlin (Cosnahan's – old surname)
Eyreton (Modern)	Eyre's town – after the owner of the land in 1867
Fleshwick (Scand)	flesvik (green creek – pronounced 'fleshik')
Foxdale (Scand)	fors (waterfall); dalr (dale)
Glen Chass (Manx)	glen (valley); shast (sedges/reeds)
Glen Dhoo (Manx)	glen (valley); dhoo (black)
Glen Needle (Manx)	glen (valley); corruption of MacNeeven
Glen Trunk (Eng)	No known reason; possibly from flotsam on the beach
Glen Wyllin (Manx)	glen (valley); mwyllin (mill)
Grenaby (Scand)	grean (green); byr (farm)
Groudle (Scand)	krappdalr; craudall (narrow glen)
Howe (Scand)	howe (mound)
Keeil ny Traie (Manx)	keeil (church); ny (of the); traie (shore)
Kerrodhoo (Manx)	kerroo (quarterland); dhoo (black – peaty ground)
Killabrega (Manx)	keeil (church); brega (Irish saint – Breaga's church)
Langness (Scand)	long promontory (long nose)
Lhiattee ny Bainnee (Manx)	lhiattee (the side); ny (of); bainnee (summit/peak)
Meayll (Mull) (Manx)	meayll (bald)
Mount Karrin (Eng/Manx)	carrin (cairn – mount of the cairn)

Niarbyl (Manx)	ny (the); arbyl (tail – of the rocks)
Perwick (Scand)	purtvik (harbour creek)
Port Grenaugh (Scand)	graenvik (green creek)
Pooyl Vaaish (Manx)	pooyl/poyll (pool/bay); vaaish (death)
Port Mooar (Manx)	Phurt Mooar (Big Port)
Port Soldrick/Soderick (Scand)	solvik (sunny creek)
Port e Vullen (Manx)	Phurt e Vullen (Port of the Mill)
Rushen (Old Eng)	rushen (rushes)
Rhyne (Manx)	rheynn (ridge)
Sartfell (Scand)	sart (dark/black); fell (mountain)
Scarlett (Scand)	skafakleft (cormorant's cleft)
Scholaby (Scand)	Skolla's byr (farm)
Skerranes (Manx)	skerraneyen (little sea-rocks)
Slieu Curn (Manx/Irish)	slieu (mountain); curn (Curryn – Curryn's mountain)
Slieu Dhoo (Manx)	slieu (mountain); dhoo (black)
Slieu Freoghane (Manx)	slieu (mountain); freoghane (bilberry/blaeberry)
Slieu Ruy (Manx)	slieu (mountain); ruy (red)
Slieu Whallian (Old Irish)	sliabh (mountain); ailin (Aylen – old surname)
Snaefell (Scand)	snae (snow); fell (mountain)
Spooyt Vane (Manx)	spooyt (spout/waterfall); vane/bane (white)
Struan ny Fasnee (Manx)	strooan (stream); ny (of); fasnee (winnowing)
Surby (Scand)	saur (moorland); byr (farm)
Tholt y Will (Manx)	tolta (hill); ny (of the); woaillee (cattle-fold)
Trollaby (Scand)	trolla (Trolli's); byr (farm)

LISTING OF CICERONE GUIDES

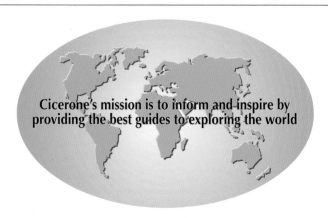

Cicerone's mission is to inform and inspire by
providing the best guides to exploring the world

Since its foundation over 30 years ago, Cicerone has specialised in publishing guidebooks and has built a reputation for quality and reliability. It now publishes nearly 300 guides to the major destinations for outdoor enthusiasts, including Europe, UK and the rest of the world.

Written by leading and committed specialists, Cicerone guides are recognised as the most authoritative. They are full of information, maps and illustrations so that the user can plan and complete a successful and safe trip or expedition – be it a long face climb, a walk over Lakeland fells, an alpine traverse, a Himalayan trek or a ramble in the countryside.

With a thorough introduction to assist planning, clear diagrams, maps and colour photographs to illustrate the terrain and route, and accurate and detailed text, Cicerone guides are designed for ease of use and access to the information.

If the facts on the ground change, or there is any aspect of a guide that you think we can improve, we are always delighted to hear from you.

Cicerone Press
2 Police Square Milnthorpe Cumbria LA7 7PY
Tel:01539 562 069   Fax:01539 563 417
e-mail:info@cicerone.co.uk   web:www.cicerone.co.uk

CICERONE